Real Life, Real Faith

Being Christian in Today's World

Bill Thomason

Judson Press ® Valley Forge

© 1994

Judson Press, Valley Forge, PA 19482-0851

Bible quotations in this volume, unless otherwise noted, are from the NEW REVISED STANDARD VERSION of the Bible, copyrighted 1989 by the Division of Christian Education of the National Council of the Churches of Christ in the United States of America, and are used by permission.

The following selections first appeared in *Pulpit Digest*:

Wishful Thinking, Fairy Tales, and the Resurrection

Annunciations

Grace and Responsibility for Creation

Soul Searching and the New Year

Value in a World of Change

A Happy New Year in the Peaceable Kingdom

The Feeding of the Five Thousand

The story *Mary's Surprise*, on pp. 23-24, is reprinted, with permission, from *Jesus for Children: Read-Aloud Gospel Stories*, copyright 1994 by William Griffin (paper, 144 pages, $9.95), published by Twenty-Third Publications, P.O. Box 180, Mystic, Ct 06355. Toll free: 1-800-321-0411.

Library of Congress Cataloging-in-Publication Data

Thomason, Bill, 1943-

Real life, real faith : being Christian in today's world / by Bill Thomason.

p. cm.

Includes bibliographical references.

ISBN 0-8170-1218-4

1. Christian life—Baptist authors. I. Title.

BV4501.2.T483 1994

248'4'861—dc2094-33708

Printed in the U.S.A.

94 95 96 97 98 99 00 01   8 7 6 5 4 3 2 1

To Bobbie

steadfast friend, faithful companion

Table of Contents

Preface

Trying to be Christian in a non-Christian world like ours can be trying. So trying, in fact, that everyone who's ever tried it has at one time or another wanted to throw in the towel, cry "uncle," refuse to answer the bell for the next round. Many do. I don't blame them—I've thrown in the towel a few times myself. Saying you're a Christian involves, at a minimum, believing in Christ (whatever that means) and trying to live out that belief in your daily life (whatever that means).

A book with a title like this one's sounds vaguely like a how-to book. How-to books are very popular and may even be helpful. However, I've never read such a book (on any subject), and I have no qualifications to write such a book (on any subject). I don't know how to do any practical thing with such expertise that it would be worth my time and effort to write a book about it or worth your money and time to buy it and read it.

Certainly, I'm no authority on how to be a Christian.

Furthermore, one thing I'm sure of is that *Christianity Made Simple in Five Easy Steps* (money back guaranteed if not completely satisfied!) is self-contradictory. Whatever Christianity is, it's not easy. And the idea that the Christian faith can be reduced to a series of steps you follow until—voila!—you have a Christian (rather like putting together a model airplane) strikes me as naive at best and blasphemous at worst.

At least some of the so-called baby-boomer religion comes dangerously close to this Christianity-by-the-numbers approach: "shopping around" for the "right church family" that will "meet our spiritual needs." What is wrong with meeting spiritual needs? Absolutely nothing. And I believe that nothing will satisfy those needs better than faith in Christ. What is wrong with this consumer approach to religion is that it starts from the wrong starting point—an emphasis on us and our needs, instead of an emphasis on God as revealed in Christ. This approach makes our faith conform to our lives, instead of our lives conform to our faith.

If this book is not going to simplify Christianity and make it easy, and if it's not going to help you find the "best value" in the "marketplace of religion," then what will it do for you? That's a good question. The answer depends to a large extent on who you are; and since I don't know who you are, I simply can't say what this book might do for you. I can say what I intended by writing it, and that may help you decide whether or not you want to continue reading.

I want to be and try to be a Christian. I do the outward things Christians are supposed to do—go to church regularly, support the church with time and money and effort, more or less obey the Ten Commandments (some less than more), and try to live up to the Sermon on the Mount, more or less. I'm not kidding myself that doing these things makes me a Christian—though if I didn't do them, I and everyone else who knows me would have reason to question my claim to be a Christian.

In addition to these Christian activities, I am also a fairly typical twentieth-century American. I have one wife, one daughter, one house, one mortgage, one car, and one dog. (On reflection, having only one of each of these items that most Americans seem to have two or more of—especially wives, children, mortgages, and cars—may mean I'm not so typical after all.) I've worked in religious publishing for the past several years and before that ran a couple of bookstores and before that taught philosophy and religion at both state-supported and denominational universities.

I grew up in a fundamentalist Southern Baptist church in Oklahoma City, Oklahoma, attended Oklahoma Baptist University (which, mercifully, helped deliver me from the worst aspects of my fundamentalist background), and did graduate work at the Southern Baptist Theological Seminary in Louisville, Kentucky (B.D. and Ph.D., but no ordination; I'm a layperson). I live in Louisville with my one wife, one daughter, one dog, etc. I am an active member of Crescent Hill Baptist Church (where, as a teacher of a young adult couples class for eleven years, I developed most of the ideas for this book). If you walked into Crescent Hill on a typical Sunday morning, not knowing it was Baptist, you might not light on "Baptist" as your first guess.

I am not relating these autobiographical details because this book is autobiographical—it is not. Other than the first chapter, which deals with the death of my father, none of these reflections are about me, except in the sense that they represent what I believe. I mention my religious faith and my personal life because my purpose in writing has been to discover the connection, if any, between the two. What difference do the study, worship, and prayer of Sunday make to me the rest of the week? If they are not making a difference, why not? I am trying to put into words what being a Christian means to me.

So, there it is. You now have to decide whether or not these occasional pieces of personal reflection on what it means to be a Christian in today's world are worth it for you to continue reading. I hope they are, and I hope you do. If you already believe, I hope these words will strengthen and confirm you in your faith. If you don't believe, I hope these words will illuminate clearly for you what it is you don't believe. And if you are somewhere in between belief and disbelief—which is most of us, at least some of the time—I hope these words will help you say, "I believe. Help my unbelief."

Acknowledgments

Writing a book is a fundamentally solitary process. The author sits alone at a desk with pen and paper staring him in the face or (more likely these days) with word processor mutely awaiting her instructions. What goes into the book, however, is the shared experience the author brings to blank paper or blinking monitor with a wide community of relatives, friends, acquaintances, role models, other books, movies, plays, and so forth. The people in this community of experience often contribute without even knowing it.

Hence, acknowledgments.

The following are the primary contributors, of whom I am aware, to the experience out of which this book grew.

Crescent Hill Baptist Church, Louisville, Kentucky: a congregation whose creative spirit fosters the gifts of its members. *Sine qua non.*

The Cornerstone Class of Crescent Hill: which I was privileged to teach for eleven years from its inception in 1980 and which provided the venue for the ideas in this book. *Sine qua non.*

Bill Johnson, minister of education at Crescent Hill: pastor, friend, colleague, and (what is all too rare these days) a minister who actually reads real books.

Some special people who graciously read the manuscript, offering comments and encouragement: Dr. Jann Aldredge-Clanton; my mother-in-law, Bonnie Williamson; Betty Cook, who wrote thoughtful notes on each chapter and, who along with my mother-in-law, exemplifies the truth of Browning's assertion, "the best is yet to be."

Some special friends who have rooted for me all the way: Diane and Rae, Mary and Steve, Gary and Judy, Dan and Eileen, Bob and Roxann (whose son Jeff will probably want to grill me about much of what I've written).

My sister, Judy Rorick, of Oklahoma City, Oklahoma: who also read this and encouraged me and who provides a quiet, pleasant place for me to stay and write when I am in Oklahoma.

Janet Hoomes: for her sharp eye that caught errors I had missed and her fast, efficient word processing skills in preparing the manuscript for Judson Press.

The staff of Judson Press: especially Kristy Arnesen Pullen (who finally reached me in Greenville, South Carolina, by phone on February 15, 1994, after our answering machines had spent two weeks talking to each other, to tell me Judson wanted to publish this), Patricia Finn, Mary Nicol, Bill Key, and Dr. Hal Rast.

An anonymous member of Crescent Hill: who, without knowing it, has become an example to me of Christian discipleship.

Frederick Buechner: whose influence permeates this book and who—in what can only be described as an Act of Grace—read this in manuscript and kept on encouraging me to find a publisher when I was ready to give up. *Sine qua non.*

And, my wife, Bobbie, and daughter, Anne: whose practical, no-nonsense attitudes are a good and necessary counterweight to my flights of fancy. *Sine qua non.*

Oklahoma City, Oklahoma
April 20, 1994

Advent and Holy Week

Birth, Death, and Last Times*

Matthew 1:18-25

I

Love, peace, hope, joy—these are the Christian realities we celebrate during Advent. And of these, joy is probably the reality we experience most fully at this time of year. During Advent we celebrate the central fact of our faith—the coming of Christ our Savior in the birth of Jesus. What other human event causes more joy than the birth of a child?

But this Advent season has been, for me, overshadowed by another central fact—the fact of death. Two weeks ago my father died of a heart attack. And so, this Advent I am living an irony. At a time when we celebrate a birth, I must come to terms with a death.

Perhaps it's not too strong to assert that death is always an irony, that it is never completely expected (even when most certain), that it always catches us by surprise (at least a little bit). Listen to what Frederick Buechner writes about the surprising, unexpected character of death:

> For every man there finally comes not just a last time but a whole calendar of last times—the last time he sees his child, his wife, his friend. The last time he takes a walk along the beach or sees the rain fall. The last time he makes love or writes a letter, builds a fire, hears his name spoken. It is part of the mercy of things that he rarely knows when each last time comes, is never sure when he is saying goodbye for good. Even the old man dying in his bed believes that he will feel the touch of a human hand

*For Joe and Debbie Williams, who gave me the idea for this book when they asked for a copy of this lesson.

2

again before he's done or hear the drawing of the blind,
smell breakfast, drift off one more time into an old man's
dozing. For some it is given to know—the criminal watch-
ing the sun come up on the morning of his execution, the
suicide writing his note—but even for them there must al-
ways be the wild hope that somehow a miracle will hap-
pen to save them.[1]

The last time I spoke with my father was about a month ago
when he phoned to tell me that he and my mother were moving
and what their new address would be as of December 3. He didn't
know and I didn't know that this would be the last time we
would ever speak to each other. He didn't know and I didn't
know that he was naming the day of his death, December 3, 1983,
the day he and my mother were moving.

I remember another last time—the last time we did anything
together, the last time really I ever saw him. It was last summer
when he and my daughter, Anne, and I went to see the Louisville
Redbirds play the Oklahoma City 89ers in Oklahoma City. Bobbie and I had decided to take our vacation in Oklahoma this year,
because (we reasoned) our parents are getting on in years; we
don't know how much longer they will live; we want Anne to
see her grandparents as much as possible, and so on.

My father was a baseball fan all of his life. In fact, part of our
family apocrypha is the story that he had once aspired to play
baseball professionally, but his mother had squelched that idea
because it meant working on Sunday. He coached some of the
teams I played on in grade school and high school. And for years
after I had left home, he continued to coach and umpire for the
Oklahoma City YMCA leagues. We had a good time at that ball
game, the three of us. He rooted for the 89ers; Anne and I rooted
for the Redbirds, and our team won in the eighth inning with a
grand slam home run.

This is the last time my father and I did anything together, and
I know we could have done a lot worse than spending that time
at a baseball game.

II

What difference would it have made if I had known this was the
last time we would see each other? What would I have said or done
differently? Our relationship had always been an oblique, indi-

rect one. Had I known we would never see each other again, I might have tried to say or do something to mark the significance of this last time together. That wouldn't have worked; it would have put a constraint on us that last time. (We already had enough of those.) Perhaps, as Buechner says, it is a mercy that we don't know when we're saying goodbye for good. Perhaps the mercy of not knowing is precisely that I did not act differently, that my daughter and father and I acted just exactly as we would have had there still been other, future times.

Death, when it is known, has the awful power to alter our behavior for the simple reason that it is so final. Whatever I might have said or done, I can't now say or do; it's too late. My father is dead, and I'll never see him again in this life. Death is the last time for anything.

But death has another power as well—the power to make us appreciate the gift of life. Because we never quite expect death and because death is the last time for anything, all of us live with the awareness that any moment may be our last. We make plans for the future, saying things like "Tomorrow I'll do this" or "Next week I'm going to do that." But we are always conscious of the Great Conditional we all live under but seldom articulate, the unspoken assumption that death will not intervene—though we all know that at any moment it could and it might.

Each moment becomes precious in the light of death because we all know that each moment is a gift we might not have had. Ordinary, mundane, apparently insignificant activities suddenly take on new meaning when we begin thinking thoughts like these. Even something as trivial as a minor-league baseball game becomes important. It becomes a requiem for a lover of baseball, a moment of fun and good feeling, the fitting finale for a life that had not always known those benefactions.

III

We can, of course, become morbid dwelling on such thoughts. Besides, there's more to say about life than that it ends in death and that death is a final separation. There is, for example, the fact of birth. What does birth tell us about life?

Well, if death reminds us that things come to an end, birth obviously reminds us that things also have a beginning. Birth reminds us of new life—because birth is the renewal of life. On the day my father died, thousands of children were born. A day full of sorrow for me and my family because of death was a day full of joy for others because of birth, because of new life in their lives. Such a realization is comforting. Life may end in death, yet it continually renews itself in birth.

But if this is all that we can say in the face of death, then I think our comfort is cold comfort indeed. Every child born the day my father died will also die one day. Every child has a birthday, but every child also has a death-day. Death is inexorable and inescapable. It will happen to us all. Birth may keep life going, but death is the final word about life. The comfort and reassurance given by the fact of birth fades into sorrow and doubt in the face of death.

And yet, here in Advent we celebrate birth, we celebrate life. Is our Christian celebration of birth and life at this time of year nothing but a vain show, a foolish and willful ignoring of the brute facts, a fearful whistling past the graveyard? Is it merely a psychological mechanism for coping with unpleasant facts we don't want to face? Is there anything to hope for beyond the hope for a life lived as fully as possible right here and now?

IV

Our gospel lesson is Matthew's account of the birth of Jesus. It goes like this:

> This is the story of the birth of the Messiah. Mary his mother was betrothed to Joseph; before their marriage she found that she was with child by the Holy Spirit. Being a man of principle, and at the same time wanting to save her from exposure, Joseph desired to have the marriage contract set aside quietly. He had resolved on this, when an angel of the Lord appeared to him in a dream. "Joseph son of David," said the angel, "do not be afraid to take Mary home with you as your wife. It is by the Holy Spirit that she has conceived this child. She will bear a son; and you will give him the name Jesus (Savior), for he will save his people from their sins." All this happened in order to fulfill what the Lord declared through the prophet: "The virgin will conceive and bear a son, and he shall be called Emmanuel, a name which means 'God is with us.'" Rising from sleep Joseph did as the angel had directed him; he took Mary home to be his wife, but had no inter-

course with her until her son was born. And he named the
child Jesus (Matthew 1:18-25, NEB).

This story in Matthew is the story of what we celebrate during this season. It is the story of a birth. And like death, birth is the most common experience of life. Like death, birth happens every day, 365 days a year. The birth of Jesus was like any other birth of any other human baby. It occurred at a specific place and time (Bethlehem in Judea, during the reign of Herod). Mary's pregnancy was nine months long, and her labor pains were real.

V

And yet, though birth in general is a common and ordinary event, this birth in particular was uncommon and extraordinary—in spite of everything it had in common with every other birth. There is, first of all, the strange manner of its beginning. A virgin conceives, and that's more than just extraordinary; that's impossible; that just doesn't happen in the ordinary course of nature. And then, there's that extraordinary man Joseph who had decided to divorce Mary quietly instead of making her a public example (as he had a right to do). This uncommon man has a troubling dream full of angels with strange messages, and on that basis he decides to trust Mary and go through with the marriage.

And the names of this child, born in these extraordinary circumstances to these extraordinary parents, are also extraordinary, indicating that the child will be extraordinary. He is to be called "Jesus" (which means "Savior," Matthew tells us parenthetically) because he will save his people from their sins (and, we add parenthetically, from the consequence of sin, which is death). And he is also to be called "Emmanuel" (which means "God with us," Matthew explains) because in him God will be fully identified with us in our humanity, including our being born and even our dying.

This birth, then, was no mere renewal of life, as wonderful as the renewal of life is. This birth, instead, is the very transformation of life into something else, something new and different, something that not even sin can touch. This newborn child is the one who will save us from our sin and all that sin means—including even death.

And so, this Advent I both grieve and celebrate at the same

time. I grieve my father's death with the finality death means, with its closing off of possibilities. Yet, I also celebrate the birth of Jesus, the Savior from sin, the one who is "God with us." If death closes off possibilities, then the birth of Jesus opens them up again, and in a richness and fullness we can scarcely begin to imagine. My celebration is greater than my grief; my loss (though great) is caught up in the hope of a greater gain.

For the one who believes in it, the birth of Jesus means that God is with us and for us and that nothing can change that—not even death itself.

Notes

1. Frederick Buechner, *The Faces of Jesus* (New York: Riverwood Publishers Limited and Simon and Schuster, 1974), 127.

Seasons of Celebration and Advent

Matthew 13:1-23

I

The Christian faith is one, yet there are many differing Christian denominations. Sorting them all out can be an act of frustration and despair. What is it that makes Russian Orthodox and Assemblies of God, Roman Catholics and Baptists, Episcopalians and Methodists, Presbyterians and Quakers all Christians? What is it that makes them all different as well? All are Christian because each attempts to live out a common commitment to Christ. All are different, however, because each of these attempts takes shape in different times and places and in response to specifically different situations. Sometimes the emergence of a new Christian group is also the result of a dominant personality, who has a particular (and to others, often, a peculiar) understanding of commitment to Christ.

One way of bringing order to this wild diversity is to categorize Christian groups according to polity (the way the group's life is organized) and worship. For example, Christian denominations can (very roughly) be divided into the hierarchical/liturgical traditions and the congregational or free church traditions. In the first instance, the church is organized from the top down, and its worship is a prescribed ritual. In the second instance, the local congregation retains the ultimate power to make decisions about its belief and practice.

The free church tradition stresses the autonomy of the local congregation (rather than ecclesiastical hierarchies) and a symbolic (rather than sacramental) understanding of worship. This is one reason why those of us in this tradition call the basic acts of the church *ordinances* instead of *sacraments*. We say they are practices ordained by Jesus to help us remember him and increase our faith and commitment but that they are only symbolic; they have no saving significance in themselves. In a similar manner, we de-emphasize the importance of special times and days and persons; in other words, we do not follow the lectionary, nor do we have officially elected saints.

Nevertheless, for all our unliturgical (and in some cases even antiliturgical) tradition, we, in fact, have developed our own special times and days and seasons of celebration. For example, the most antiliturgical churches of our tradition will, in spite of their abhorrence of anything smacking of liturgy, nevertheless begin singing Advent and Christmas music in the four weeks preceding Christmas Day. And I doubt that any of these churches fail to observe those days of special emphasis that come around like clockwork each year—for example, the Spring Revival. In other words, we do have a church calendar, whether or not we call it that and whether or not we want to admit it.

In addition, we even have our "saints," whom we revere just as much as Catholics revere theirs. We have Lottie Moon and Annie Armstrong, Dwight L. Moody and Charles G. Finney, Adoniram Judson and William Carey. (And, undoubtedly, one day when it is seemly to do so, we will inscribe Billy Graham's name in that small pantheon.) Of course, we don't pray to our saints or ask for their intercession, but we do revere them and celebrate their lives and tell their stories as models of good Christian behavior.

The lesson in all this, I think, is that seasons of celebration—special times when we focus our attention on special concerns and people—are necessary and inevitable. We *need* such seasons and cannot really escape them. If we reject one kind of celebration (say, the liturgical celebrations of the Catholic tradition), we will turn right around and create some of our own. In short, we human beings are destined to celebrate those things that are most important to us, so special seasons are necessary and inescapable.

II

This need for ceremony, ritual, and the regular observance of celebration pervades all of human life, even the most secular. No sports championship, for example, can ever occur without marching bands, fireworks, and entertainment by the biggest big-name star it's possible to get. The Olympic Games begin with the impressive ceremony of the Olympic torch being carried into the stadium. We remember birthdays with cards and cakes and presents. And woe to the spouse who forgets a wedding anniversary or the lover who forgets Valentine's Day!

All of these are merely secular ceremonies, yet they raise a serious question for us—namely, why have *religious* ceremonies? Why not simply satisfy our human need for celebration with these secular rites? Our secular rites, in fact, seem to be sufficient for a large number of Americans, who may claim to be religious in some sense but who hardly ever worship or otherwise participate in religious activities. The ritual of a leisurely reading of the Sunday paper over a second cup of coffee seems to be about the only ceremony most Americans want on Sunday mornings. So, why bother to celebrate at church with religious ceremonies if all of us are quite capable of creating our own ceremonies suited to our own needs?

Besides, religion really can discomfit us, make us squirm, touch some touchy subjects, confront us with things we would rather not be confronted with. In fact, religion can be so disturbing of our self-satisfaction at times that I wonder how anyone could ever construe it as wish-fulfillment. If I were creating my own religion out of my own desires and wishes and hopes, I never would have included demands such as loving my enemies or doing good for people I can't stand and who can't stand me. So, the question stands: Why *religious* ceremonies? What is different about them that makes them unique and necessary;why are they celebrations that no merely secular rite could ever adequately supplant?

III

The Christian answer to this question involves us with one of the basic doctrines of our faith—the doctrine of creation. The first article of the Apostle's Creed—"I believe in God the Father Almighty, Creator of heaven and earth"—is our way of saying that God is the ultimate reality and that everything else is the creation of that ultimate reality. This doctrine is our way of saying that God is the source of all that is and that everything that is ultimately depends on God for its existence. This doctrine, however, is not just, or even primarily, about origins, about the literal beginning of things. It is, rather, primarily about the present existence of everything. The doctrine of creation is our way of saying that *at every moment* everything depends on God and that without God's continuous, sustaining activity (at this and every moment), the universe would instantly collapse back into the nothingness from which it was created.

This basic belief has a very important implication for us. Namely, we are always in the presence of God, the Creator; we can never escape from the reality of God which surrounds us; every moment of our existence is sustained by God's ever-present activity. Here's how Thomas Merton put it:

> *Every moment and every event of every man's life on earth plants something in his soul. For just as the wind carries thousands of invisible and visible winged seeds, so the stream of time brings with it germs of spiritual vitality that come to rest imperceptibly in the minds and wills of men. Most of these unnumbered seeds perish and are lost, because men are not prepared to receive them. . . . [But if] I were looking for God, every event and every moment would sow, in my will, grains of His life, that would spring up one day in a tremendous harvest.[1]*

"Every moment and every event . . . plants something in [the] soul," Merton wrote. And if we were serious in looking for God, then every event and moment and experience we have would sow in our lives something of God's reality, some divine germ of life that would one day produce a bountiful spiritual harvest. As Jesus said in the parable of the sower, ". . . the seed that fell into good soil is the one who hears the word and understands it, who accordingly bears fruit, and yields a hundredfold, or, it may be, sixtyfold or thirtyfold." Merton's point is simple. Because God is the Creator of everything and because God is ever active in sustaining the universe at every moment of its existence, then every moment is potentially an epiphany, a moment when we could see God, when God's reality could become reality for us.

IV

If all the foregoing is in some way true, then it would help explain why we have special seasons of celebration. Merton also wrote, "Most of these unnumbered seeds perish and are lost, because [we] are not prepared to receive them." In other words, we have special seasons of the year in order to prepare ourselves in special ways for God's ever-present coming to us. God is always present in our lives, but we seem to have a genius for missing this divine presence. A special season of celebration is like a farmer tilling the ground; without such preparation most of the seed would be lost, but with it the seed may germinate and grow to a bountiful harvest.

The free church tradition embodies one part of the truth we are struggling with here—namely, that every moment and place and person is holy and sacred so that none should be any more special than any other. But the liturgical traditions have embodied another part of the truth that we in the free church tradition could profit from hearing—namely, that we usually miss these always-possible epiphanies and that special seasons in which we focus our lives on God's reality are ways of helping us nourish the growth of God's reality within us.

One of the wisest creations of the church was the church calendar, the liturgical year, which divides the chronological year up into special seasons of celebration. Roman Catholics, Episcopalians, Lutherans, Presbyterians, and Methodists all (with variations) follow this calendar. The church year begins with Advent, moves into Christmas, Epiphany, Lent, and Easter and culminates in Pentecost. It is the calendar of "the year of our Lord, Jesus Christ." And what it really does is tell a story—the story of redemption, the story of what God has done to save us from our sins. The church determines its life by this story (whether or not it follows the calendar). And in proclaiming this story, the life of the church becomes a part of that story. The church becomes an agent of redemption, continuing the work that Christ began. In other words, the church calendar, the liturgical year, is a way to proclaim the Gospel; it's a means of evangelism.

Seen in this light, the liturgical year is not really all that foreign to the free church traditions. We have taken seriously the responsibility of evangelism, and the drama of salvation embodied in the church calendar is one very powerful method we could use to proclaim the gospel. "Tell me the story of Jesus/Write on my heart every word," we are fond of singing; "Tell me the story most precious/Sweetest that ever was heard." The church calendar *is* the sweet story of Jesus, and we should not be afraid to use it as one way we have to evangelize.

V

With all this in mind, we come to this first season of celebration, the season of Advent, in which we prepare ourselves for the coming of Christ. That's what Advent means—"to come to" or "to come near, to approach." It carries the connotation of expectancy—the advent of something is the coming of something we were expecting. But what is expected may not arrive on time or may not arrive at all. It may be delayed or hindered or stopped altogether from coming. Hence, the word *advent* is related to the word *adventure*, which means "a bold undertaking involving hazards, risks, and an uncertain outcome." Furthermore, the outcome of an adventure is important, crucial, a matter of life and death to those who undertake it. So, with an adventure there is an air of expectancy yet uncertainty because there is also danger and risk.

During Advent we who are Christians begin the celebration of the greatest adventure of all—the coming of God in Christ to save a lost world. Like every adventure, it has the qualities we've just noticed—risk, danger, hazard, but also expectancy, hope, and joy. And we who celebrate Advent participate in that divine adventure with all of its drama and uncertainty and hopefulness. The world may reject what God is doing to save it from its sin. And that means the world may reject us too and the story we tell and live. There weren't any guarantees that anyone would listen to Jesus, and there aren't any guarantees that anyone will listen to us either.

But a special season such as this, in which we dramatize the Christian story in our worship, may intrigue the world, may spark some interest, may cause the world to take a second look at the story it has so casually been dismissing or ignoring. For that matter, such seasons of celebration may make us stop and pay attention once again to the "old, old story," which, because it is so old and familiar to us, may have lost its excitement and freshness and ability to renew our lives.

We are inherently inclined to celebrate by our very natures as human beings. Our merely secular celebrations won't satisfy our deepest, most human needs. But the Christian story, embodied in our Christian calendar, does satisfy those longings. This is the season of Advent, the beginning of the Christian adventure.

Let's celebrate!

Notes

1. Thomas Merton, *Seeds of Contemplation* (Norfolk, Conn.: New Directions Books, 1949), 17-18.

Wishful Thinking, Fairy Tales, and the Resurrection

Mark 16:1-8

I

"Christianity is mainly wishful thinking," Frederick Buech-ner writes in a book entitled *Wishful Thinking.*[1] And in another book he writes a whole chapter on "The Gospel as Fairy Tale."[2] Surely, in our modern, skeptical age that is what most people seem to think about religion in general and Christianity in particular. Christianity is wishful thinking. According to Ludwig Feuerbach, it's nothing but the projection of our own deepest hopes and desires onto the universe. We make God in our own image, instead of the other way around. And the easiest way to dismiss the claims of religion on us (if dismissing the claims of religion on us is what we want to do) is to say that religion is a fairy tale, a myth, an old wives' tale (though I suspect old wives' tales may be no less true for being the stories of elderly matrons).

If anything seems to prove that Christianity is wishful think-ing or a fairy tale, it would be the Gospel narratives of the Resurrection. Surely the disciples wanted to believe that Jesus was not really dead. And doesn't that explain why they came to believe in the Resurrection? Didn't their wish conceive and give birth to their thought? Since they wanted to believe that Jesus was not really dead, they fooled themselves into believing he was alive. Now, some members of the AAAA (American Asso-ciation for the Advancement of Atheism) get properly scandal-ized about this—as if the disciples deliberately set out first to deceive themselves and then to deceive the whole world. How-ever, most people these days take a more benign and sympathetic

15

view of this Christian benightedness. Knowing what we know about the unconscious and the subconscious, we today can be sympathetic to the plight of the disciples. They were grieving, after all, and the mind can do strange things in times of stress. So, most of us are willing to be tolerant of the disciples, seeing their belief in the Resurrection as understandable wish fulfillment, the projection of their own deepest longings and desires. Nevertheless, if anything seems to prove that religion in general and Christianity in particular is wishful thinking, the Christian belief in the Resurrection of Christ on Easter Sunday seems to turn the trick.

Furthermore, if you know a little bit about the Bible, this modern attitude toward the Resurrection is reinforced because the Gospel accounts don't agree with one another in the details of their narratives. Matthew, for example, speaks of two women coming to the tomb on Easter morning—Mary Magdalene and Mary the mother of James and Joseph. But Mark speaks of three women (those in Matthew, plus a woman named Salome), while Luke has an indeterminate number of women, and John says only Mary Magdalene was there. Matthew and Mark have one angel at the tomb (and Mark doesn't call him an angel but rather a young man); Luke and John have two. When Matthew's angel descends from heaven, there's an earthquake that the other three Evangelists somehow missed. These stories don't agree in all their details, and this proves to modern, up-to-date people that they can't be true. (Perhaps it also proves the dangers of knowing only a little about the Bible.)

In addition to these discrepancies of detail, there is also the temptation to intellectual skepticism concerning the possibility of miracles. The temper of our times, in general, is against believing in miraculous events that can't be explained in terms of the laws of nature. Such skepticism is simply a part of the cultural air we breathe, and we don't have to have majored in philosophy or physics to know (or think we know) that miracles can't happen.

II

But let me suggest one other stumbling block on our path to believing in the Resurrection—namely, the moral cynicism of our day. A cynic is a disappointed, disenchanted idealist who once believed that good was to be preferred over evil, that right was better than wrong, and that choosing the good and right would actually make a difference. The cynic no longer believes these things. His or her idealism has been battered to bits on the rough reef of reality and has become nothing but flotsam and jetsam on the sea of the cynic's life. Every particular cynic's biography will differ as to detail, but the general pattern is the same: High ideals that continually get battered down and trampled on, often by the very people who are supposed to uphold them. Finally that happens once too often, and the idealist (weary of fighting what seems to be eternally lost causes) turns into a cynic and says, "Why should I care, why should I beat my brains out for what I believe in when nobody else seems to care?" So, a cynic who reads a story about someone doing good—someone telling the truth, say, when it would have been easier to lie—knows deep down inside that there was a payoff somewhere. People just aren't that good.

And this is why, for many people, the Resurrection narratives sound so unbelievable, so incredible. This is why the Resurrection has such a fairy tale quality about it, why it seems to be such a fine example, a paradigm case, of wishful thinking. For the Resurrection of Jesus is the story of the triumph of good over evil, right over wrong. And the cynic is the one who has given up believing that such things can happen. Think, for a moment, of all the evils arrayed against Jesus in the Crucifixion—misunderstanding, betrayal, political oppression, injustice, religious hypocrisy, irrationality, ambition, pride, arrogance —all these and more were there nailing Jesus to the cross. The Resurrection reversed all these evils and their effects. Life won out over death; good triumphed over evil. And the cynic, who once believed this sort of thing but then got burned once too often, dismisses such a story as a fairy tale, a bit of wishful thinking.

III

And yet, in spite of all this modern, up-to-date outlook that we breathe in as a part of our cultural atmosphere, there's something in us that doesn't quite want to accept this outlook, modern and up-to-date though it may be. We are a little bit like the speaker of Thomas Hardy's poem "The Oxen":

Christmas Eve, and twelve of the clock.
  "Now they are all on their knees,"
An elder said as we sat in a flock
  By the embers in hearthside ease.

We pictured the meek mild creatures where
  They dwelt in their strawy pen,
Nor did it occur to one of us there
  To doubt they were kneeling then.

So fair a fancy few would weave
  In these years! Yet, I feel,
If someone said on Christmas Eve,
  "Come; see the oxen kneel,

"In the lonely barton by yonder coomb
  Our childhood used to know,"
I should go with him in the gloom,
  Hoping it might be so.[3]

Hardy is, of course, satirizing the nostalgic desire for a simpler, more innocent time. Nevertheless, no matter how modern we may be, there is something in us that wants to believe that on midnight of Christmas Eve, oxen kneel in their pens, acknowledging the birth of the Savior. And the same applies to the Resurrection. No matter how up-to-date we may be, we *want* to believe in the Resurrection because it is the story of the ultimate triumph of good over evil. If it is true, it would be, to use the jargon of Hollywood, the Greatest Story Ever Told.

This "and yet" should give us pause. Maybe we need to rethink our modern skepticism. Are the discrepancies in the Resurrection narratives really that important? Whatever else they may prove, they certainly don't prove that the Resurrection didn't occur. Think about the points on which they agree: Mary Magdalene was there; the tomb was empty; at least one angel told Mary to tell the disciples that Jesus had been raised from the dead and was alive. The Gospel accounts, in other words, agree on the major points. And they further agree that Jesus himself appeared to some of his disciples and that there was no doubt about who it was. The risen Christ could be seen and heard; he could be touched. He could eat food. In John's Gospel he even cooks a meal and feeds his bewildered, confused disciples, who can't quite believe their eyes but do believe their hearts, which beat with wild, joyous recognition that this is indeed Jesus, who had died. The discrepancies in the Gospel accounts are all the more reason for believing in the authenticity of these narratives. These diverse accounts—agreeing on the main points but disagreeing in detail—are precisely what we should expect to find in accounts of such an incident witnessed under such circumstances.

And with regard to our intellectual skepticism: Why are we so sure that miracles can't happen? The widespread disbelief in miracles is one of our modern prejudices. And like all prejudices, we ought to examine this one to see if it has any validity. We cannot undertake a full examination here. Let it suffice to say that the two most perceptive and apt critics of religious miracles—David Hume in the eighteenth century and his twentieth century disciple, Antony Flew—are both guilty of logical errors in their arguments. Hume says that on strictly empiricist grounds anything is a possibility; then he turns around and denies the possibility of miracles. And Flew begs the question when he asserts that anything that does in fact happen is, ipso facto, a natural event regardless of how contrary it may be to the "ordinary course of nature."

And finally, I have already pointed out that beneath our moral cynicism there is probably a deep yearning to believe in the triumph of good over evil and, therefore, a deep yearning to believe the stories of the Resurrection. What, then, did Buechner mean when he wrote that "Christianity is mainly wishful thinking" and when he likened the Gospel to a fairy tale?

IV

The answer is that Buechner was leading us on in order to lead us in—to lead us into a deeper understanding of the Gospel, that is. I didn't quote all he wrote about Christianity as wishful thinking. Here's the full quote:

> *Christianity is mainly wishful thinking. Even the part about Judgment and Hell reflects the wish that somewhere the score is being kept.*
> *Dreams are wishful thinking. Children playing at being grown-up is wishful thinking. Interplanetary travel is wishful thinking.*
> *Sometimes wishing is the wings the truth comes true on. Sometimes the truth is what sets us wishing for it.*[4]

Wishful thinking isn't necessarily wishing for the moon. Sometimes, it's wishing for the truth, and sometimes it's the truth that sets off our wishful thinking. To tell stories about the triumph of good over evil is wishful thinking. But maybe it's the kind of wishful thinking set in motion by the truth that good is, in fact, triumphing over evil. Maybe one of the problems of our day, maybe one of the reasons evil seems so powerful today is that we have not engaged in enough wishful thinking about overcoming evil. "Sometimes wishing is the wings the truth comes true on," Buechner writes.

Buechner's calling the Gospel wishful thinking is really wordplay, a sort of joke. Let's call it a holy joke. Certainly God engaged in some wishful thinking in sending Jesus to save the world. Jesus was a kind of "holy joke" because no one is his or her right mind would ever think, just by looking at him, that Jesus was the Savior of the world. We want *our* savior to look like Robert Redford. We would have had the savior born in Rome in the imperial household, where he could save the world by wise and rational political means. Or better yet, we would have had the savior born in *our* century, when he could beam his message around the world via worldwide telecommunications networks, capturing the widest distribution and the largest market share of religious broadcasting.

Jesus just doesn't seem to be a savior. But then this is precisely one of the characteristics of a fairy tale—things never are what they seem to be. In a fairy tale, a frog is really a handsome prince, an old wardrobe is really the entrance to an enchanted world, the beautiful queen is really an old hag, a pumpkin is really a magnificent coach, a house of gingerbread is really a death trap for little children, and so on. And fairy tales usually tell stories that are dark and dangerous. Fairy tails pull no punches. Cruelty is right up front for anyone to see, even little children. Danger and death occur all the time in fairy tales. They are not all sweetness and light. But again, this is exactly true of the gospel. As Buechner says, the gospel is bad news before it is good news.[5] It's the bad news about all of us—that we are sinners and we are lost, not knowing the way to go, and that we need a savior.

V

But if fairy tales are dark, they are also full of light, because in a fairy tale good finally does triumph over evil, in spite of the odds against it. The witch is pushed into the oven, not Hansel and Gretel. Prince Charming does finally find Cinderella among the cinders, in spite of the efforts of the wicked stepmother and stepsisters to keep her hidden. Beauty goes back to the Beast because she really does love him in spite of his ugliness, and the Beast turns out to be a handsome prince whose curse of ugliness could only be lifted by someone truly loving him. And in every case, in a fairy tale "they lived happily ever after." Buechner says that fairy tales are essentially stories of transformation. "From darkness riseth light," the psalmist wrote, "light to the upright." And the transformation in a fairy tale from darkness to light is such that in the end all creatures are revealed for what they truly are— whether truly good or truly bad, truly beautiful or truly ugly, truly just or truly wicked. And this transformation of every creature in a fairy tale for what it really and truly is creates an ache in us, a longing that it be so. If only living happily ever after and if only the triumph of good over evil were true, we say wistfully to ourselves.

But they *are* true. The gospel differs from fairy tales in one important respect—unlike fairy tales, it really happened in history. The gospel happened once upon a time, when Augustus was Caesar and Pontius Pilate was procurator of Judea. Jesus really walked the same earth you and I walk. He taught people in parables, performed miracles, died on a cross, and God raised him from the dead on the third day. The ache, the longing, the yearning for joy and goodness we feel when we hear a fairy tale comes true in the death and resurrection of Jesus. It really happened.

But this is not all. It not only happened "once upon a time" back in ancient history. It keeps happening still. To tell the gospel is to tell the truth—both of what did happen on that first Easter Sunday and of what continues to happen even today, even now, even in us.

"Christ is risen. He is risen indeed!"

Notes

1. Frederick Buechner, *Wishful Thinking: A Theological ABC* (New York: Harper & Row, Publishers, 1973), 96.

2. Frederick Buechner, *Telling the Truth: The Gospel as Tragedy, Comedy, and Fairy Tale* (New York: Harper & Row, Publishers,

1977), 73-98.

3. Walter E. Houghton and G. Robert Stange, *Victorian Poetry and Poetics* (Boston: Houghton Mifflin Co., 1959), 787-788.

4. Buechner, *Wishful Thinking*, 96.

5. Buechner, *Telling the Truth*, 7.

Annunciations

Luke 1:26-38

I

This familiar story in Luke 1 is the one we usually call the Annunciation to Mary. But perhaps this term *annunciation* is misleading. To announce something means to declare what is, in fact, the case or what will be the case. Announcements concern things that are set and certain, things that are accomplished facts. This term, in other words, implies that Mary had no choice in this matter, that the angel simply told her that she was going to be the mother of Jesus, that what she may have wanted didn't matter.

Now the problem with this is that it seems out of character with other parts of the Bible that portray God as giving us freedom of choice, free will. The main thrust of the Bible, I believe, is to show us in relation to God in such a way that we may either say yes or no when there's something God wants us to do. As a consequence, I want to read another version of this story, which may help us understand this moment in Mary's life. It's a story called "Mary's Surprise" from a book by William Griffin entitled *Jesus for Children*. The story goes like this:

> "Stay where you are," said the young girl, "or I'll scream!"
> "My name is Gabriel," said the tall stranger.
> "Are you an angel?" asked Mary.
> "I have a message for you."
> "You shouldn't go about surprising people," said Mary closing her book.
> "Angels are for surprises," said Gabriel.
> "I didn't know that," said Mary.
> "You are one of God's favorites," said Gabriel. "He wants

23

you to know that."
"Thank you for telling me."
"And he wants to ask you a favor. He wants you to be the
mother of his child. The child the Scriptures speak of. The
child that will save all the people of the world. Will you do
God this favor?"
"Does he have to ask?"
"God always asks."
"He knows I read the Scriptures and will do what he asks."
"Blessed are you among women," said Gabriel, and the an-
gel was gone.
Yes, God did have to ask, thought Mary as she returned to
her book, and yes, she would never say no.[1]

II

This second version of the story of the Annunciation stresses something that I believe is very important throughout the Bible—in fact, it may be the most important thing the Bible teaches us—namely, the God of the Bible is a God who does not force the divine will on us but rather asks. God has to ask, when it comes to human beings. Now it's true that God is a God of great power, so much so that we have a formal theological term for it. We say that God is *omnipotent*. Yet, in this second version of the story, Mary says, "Does God have to ask?" And the angel responds, "God always asks." God's all-powerfulness has certain limits, set by God to be sure, but nevertheless real. The God of the Bible is a God who has to ask, when it comes to you and me.

It would seem that the story in Luke doesn't really teach us this about God—after all, the angel says, ". . . you shall conceive and bear a son and you shall call his name Jesus," and so on. This seems pretty definite and certain. It doesn't seem that Mary really has much say in the matter at all. But to interpret the story this way is to miss the whole point of this narrative, which is to lead us to the climactic moment when Mary finally responds and gives her consent: "Here am I," she says, "I am the Lord's servant; as you have spoken, so be it."

The point Luke is making here is that Mary didn't have to say yes, that the angel's announcement was conditional on what Mary would say. And clearly, the implication of Luke's story is that Mary could have said no. The point of the narrative is to focus on Mary's response—will she say yes or will she say no; will she cooperate with God in God's plan or refuse? Her response is a voluntary one: "Here am I, so be it."

III

Griffin's version emphasizes something else about God—namely, God is a "God of Surprises." After Mary got over her initial fright, she took the angel to task. "You shouldn't go about surprising people," she says. And Gabriel responds, "Angels are for surprises."

This idea of Mary's being surprised is also implicit in Luke's version. Mary was "deeply troubled" by the angel's greeting and wondered what the greeting might mean. But, of course, the most surprising thing was the angel's message. How could she have a baby since she was a virgin? If she was going to have a baby, that really would be a surprise since there was no humanly possible way for her to be pregnant. God was asking a very surprising favor from her, surprising largely because it was impossible.

We hardly need to mention that it is surprising that God would even consider Mary. She was one of the common poor people of the land. She was from Galilee, and Galilee was about as far away from the centers of power as it was possible to be. Certainly it was surprising for God to come to such a person in such a situation to make such a surprising request. But then, surprises are what angels are all about, Gabriel says.

IV

But there's one other point in Griffin's story, a point connected with that little detail that Mary was reading when the angel full of surprises appeared. Remember that Mary closed her book when she upbraided the angel for going about surprising people. And remember that when Gabriel left, Mary reflected that, "Yes, God did have to ask, . . . as she returned to her book. . . ." In other words, this momentous announcement came in the midst of ordinary, everyday life. Mary was going about her ordinary routine when the angel appeared, and after the angel left, she resumed her ordinary routine. She picked up her reading where she had been interrupted.

Now, it's true that the angel's message was very unusual and surprising. But the delivery of the message was extraordinary in its ordinariness. The angel was simply a tall stranger. The interview occurred in an ordinary human house. There were no bright lights or fireworks; the earth didn't tremble and shake. And when it was all over, Mary calmly and reflectively went back to reading her book. The God who had such a message delivered is quite clearly the "God of the Everyday and the Ordinary."

Of course, the Bible doesn't say that Mary was reading a book or that she was doing anything else for that matter. But it does mention one small detail that supports this contention that God is a God of the Ordinary and the Everyday. Luke says that the angel "went in"—meaning that Gabriel entered Mary's house by the door. He didn't suddenly materialize like Captain Kirk in "Star Trek," being transported from the *Enterprise* to the surface of some planet. The angel "went in" without knocking and interrupted whatever it was Mary was doing. Maybe, instead of reading, she was washing the dishes or sweeping the floor or sewing patches on worn clothing or baking bread. Maybe she *was* reading, for all we know. The point is that she was going about her everyday affairs so that the angel had to interrupt her, had to walk into her house, in order to deliver the message.

Well, this simple story about Jesus written for children turns out to be fraught with heavy theological weight. We have seen that God is a God who has to ask us when there's something for us to do, that God won't force the divine will upon us. And we've seen that what God asks is often very surprising and unexpected and out of the ordinary. It may even seem impossible or, perhaps, just pointless at times. (Remember in *The Karate Kid* how Mr. Miyagi insisted that Daniel paint the fence as the first step in learning karate?) And finally, we've seen that, surprisingly enough, these surprising, extraordinary requests come in the most ordinary and mundane of ways. A strange man walked into Mary's house, interrupting her housework or reading, and asked her if she'd consent to be the mother of the Messiah.

V

We tend to think that the people in the Bible were unique individuals, with all sorts of special endowments and extraordinary talents. But that's not true all the time in every case. God uses ordinary people to do extraordinary jobs, and Mary was as ordinary a person as we can find in the Bible. In fact, I wonder if Mary was the only woman Gabriel approached? I wonder if there may not have been other annunciations that we don't know about. The difference between these hypothetical annunciations and the one to Mary would be that Mary was the one to say yes.

I suspect there may have been more than one young woman in Galilee who was approached by this tall stranger. And I suspect that a lot of them thought he was crazy and told their friends to be on the lookout for this tall guy. "You can't be too careful, you know," one would say to another, "though you've got to admit that he's got a pretty original line." There probably were lots of women in Galilee who could have been the mother of the Messiah. But Mary had this honor because she said yes to Gabriel's message. As the Bible says in another place, "Many are called, but only a few are chosen"—which means only a few choose to say yes to the call.

In light of this speculation, I would like to think that you and I experience our own annunciations, in the same way Mary did. Now, you may protest that you and I are not called like Mary to bring the Savior into the world. Well, maybe not, maybe not like Mary. But in another sense, of course, God *does* ask us to do just that—God asks us to bring Christ into our own individual worlds. We call ourselves "Christians," and that means "little Christs." A Christian is one whose life imitates, reflects, embodies, shows forth (however we want to put it) the life of Christ. We give life to Christ by our actual living in concrete, specific situations— just as surely as Mary gave Jesus biological life. We do, in fact, bring Christ into the world every day of our lives by the way we live out the gospel.

That means that every day there's the possibility that we may be confronted by an angel who has an announcement to make to us. Our annunciations, like Mary's, will, of course, be surprising and unexpected. They may even seem impossible or at least slightly crazy. And part of the craziness of our annunciations will be that they will come in the midst of the ordinary events of life—as we engage in housework or business or maybe even play.

Our world is full of annunciations, if we would just open our eyes to them. But if we open our eyes to the ways God approaches us and asks us to bring Christ into the world, we must be prepared also to respond. Like Mary, we can say either yes or no—God won't make us conceive and bring Christ to life within us and within our worlds.

God is a God who has to ask.

Notes

1. From a book by William Griffin, *Jesus for Children: Read-Aloud Gospel Stories* (Twenty-Third Publications, Mystic, CT 06355).

The Post-Resurrection, Pre-Eschatological Fish Fry and Bake-off

John 21:1-25

I

We are all aware, at least vaguely, that the Gospel of John is a strange Gospel in comparison with Matthew, Mark, and Luke. If *strange* is too strong a word, then let's substitute the word *different.* John's Gospel is different from the other three Gospels. It has a different order of events, tells many stories about Jesus the other Gospels don't relate, and in general has a very different tone and style about it. The way it ends in Chapter 21 is no exception to this general rule. In fact, nowhere is the strange quality of John more manifest than in this chapter—an odd, puzzling story even for John.

One of the odd things about Chapter 21 is its tone, which is in marked contrast to the rest of John. John starts out with a lofty theological hymn to the Logos, the Word, which was incarnate in Jesus of Nazareth. "In the beginning was the Word," this Gospel begins, "and the Word was with God, and the Word was God." Every event in John's Gospel is suffused with this profound theological quality, even the most ordinary or mundane happenings. It's true that in this Gospel Jesus talks a lot about ordinary, mundane things, such as eating and drinking, being born and dying. But it's also true that Jesus never talks about merely these things, for Jesus talks about eating the *bread of life* (not just bread), drinking *living water* (not just water), being *born again* of the Spirit (not just being born once of the flesh), and of a dying that *brings forth life* (rather than the dying that brings life to an end). In this Gospel the implicit tone of the writing conveys the idea that no event has a simple, literal meaning. The simplest event—the most mundane conversation, for example, like the one with the woman at the well—resonates with undertones and overtones of meaning that no doctor of theology has yet fully sounded.

John 21, in contrast, seems to lack this profound theological quality found in the rest of the Gospel. In some ways it seems like a simple, literal story, to be taken in a straightforward way. John conveys this sense of literalness through some of the details he mentions—he identifies five of the seven disciples (and specifies that there were seven), he counts the fish so we know there were exactly 153 of them, Jesus cooks over a charcoal fire, and so on.

But in another sense, John 21 seems quite different from the rest of the Gospel because it's not a simple, literal story at all. Instead, in some ways it's a whopping tall tale. And if we had to identify its literary genre, we could make a strong case for calling it a fish story. Fish stories, as you know, are the tall tales anglers tell about "The One That Got Away" or "The Biggest Fish I Ever Caught." Each time the story gets told, the fish gets bigger and bigger until you're absolutely convinced it was the piscatological equivalent of World War II. Looked at from this perspective, John 21 certainly exhibits some of the essential characteristics of a fish story. Peter and the other disciples had nothing else to do, so they decided to go fishing one more time, for old time's sake. They worked hard all night without success; then they caught a load of fish that must have challenged all the fishing records for the Sea of Galilee in the first half of the first century. They caught 153 big fish, John says (in a fish story, the fish are always big), so many that they had trouble getting them to shore. Can anybody top that one!

On the one hand, John 21 seems to be a simple, literal story added to the Gospel to tie up a few loose ends about Peter. And on the other hand, it seems to be a whopping fish story, a tall tale designed to challenge the reader's imagination and test credulity. In either case, John 21 appears to be devoid of theological significance.

II

To add to our sense of wonder about this chapter, our questioning of exactly what it's doing in this Gospel, is the fact that it is also the story of a party, a beach party at that. John 21 tells how Jesus threw a party for his disciples on the shores of the Sea of Galilee, probably the last party he ever gave them. You may protest that this sounds absurd, trivial, even frivolous. This is Holy Scripture, after all; and we should take it seriously, not flippantly.

Perhaps so. But consider the following. We throw a party when we want to celebrate something, whether it's significant or frivolous. We like to party, for example, when we've finished working for the day, especially if it's Friday, especially if our hard work has finally paid off. Or, for another example, we like to party when friends we haven't seen in a while show up and we're eager to share some time with them. All of us have had conversations like this:

"Did you know the Hobbs and the Spears are going to be in town this weekend?"

"No, that's great. How long has it been since we've seen them?"

"Oh, I don't know, at least a couple of years."

"That long! You know, we ought to have a little party, invite a few couples over, catch up on what's happening."

"Good idea. The Zimmers would like to see them again, and so would the Crows, if they're going to be in town."

Now, I submit to you that both of these occasions for having a party characterize this story in John 21. The disciples had been working hard all night, and finally their efforts had paid off beyond their wildest expectations. That catch of fish was something to celebrate. And furthermore, their nets weren't even broken, so they did not have to do the tedious, time-consuming but necessary job of mending the nets—another reason to celebrate. And even more important, the stranger on the shore giving fishing tips was not a stranger at all, but Jesus, the one who had meant the most to them, who had been taken from them, and who had then been miraculously restored to them. The best friend they ever had was in town again, and wouldn't it be nice if they could all get together for a little party? What better reason to have a party than the reunion with an old and dear friend.

When we realize that this story is the story of a party as well as a whopping fish story, we are once again struck by its strangeness. We can't help but wonder just what it's doing at the end of John's Gospel.

III

Now it's possible that everything I've said so far is way off base, that I'm missing the point somehow. I may be guilty of eisegesis here, instead of exegesis. That is, I may be reading into the text what I want to find there instead of reading out of the text what is actually there. Maybe I've been reading too much Robert Farrar Capon, who likens God's creation to a grand party inviting all creatures to attend and enjoy it. So, maybe everything I've said so far is the Gospel according to Capon rather than the Gospel according to John. Maybe. But there are some hints in the text itself that suggest I may not be all that far off base.

The first hint occurs in verses two and three, where John names the disciples who went on this fishing trip. Five of them are identified—Peter, Thomas, Nathaniel, and the two sons of Zebedee, James and John. The other two disciples remain anonymous, and I suspect they are mentioned simply for the sake of historical veracity. Why, then, are these five specifically identified? Peter is probably mentioned because he suggested the fishing trip in the first place, and the literal level of the story concerns some unfinished business between Jesus and him. James and John are there because they, along with Peter, were the inner circle of Jesus' disciples, and they had been fishing partners of Peter's long before Jesus ever entered their lives. Thomas is there, I suspect, because he had missed one of the post-Resurrection appearances, was consequently tagged with the name "Doubting Thomas," and had vowed never to be absent again when there was the possibility that Jesus might appear. (Here I admit I'm just guessing.)

In other words, four of the five disciples named are well-known to us, and the fact that they are well-known helps account for the fact that they are named. But Nathaniel is one of the obscure disciples of Jesus about whom we know very little. Why, then, does John go to the trouble of mentioning him by name, especially since he omits the names of the other two disciples who were there? The answer is in that detail

John supplies that Nathaniel was from Cana in Galilee. Clearly, we are supposed to remember that Jesus performed his first miracle there. And the occasion for that miracle was a wedding feast—that is, a celebration, a party—where the host had run out of wine and was about to be socially humiliated. The party would be ruined without more wine, so Jesus turned water into wine and saved the party and its host. And according to John, it was good wine, too, none of this $1.98 Thunderbird firewater, none of this wine cooler business that's suddenly gotten so popular. No, at this party Jesus turned ordinary water into the first-century Jewish equivalent of Chateau Lafitte-Rothschild, vintage 1928.

Now, once we begin thinking in these terms, we can find lots of parties in John's Gospel, that is, lots of occasions when people ate and drank together, not just for nourishment but for celebration. The wedding at Cana in Galilee is the most obvious example. But there's also the feeding of the five thousand in John 6. Remember on that occasion Jesus took five loaves of bread and two fish and turned those meager resources into a feast so abundant and rich that the disciples collected twelve baskets of gourmet leftovers. (Perhaps John was alluding to this party when he stated in 21:9 that Jesus was preparing fish and bread.) Remember also that John's Gospel is structured around a series of feasts, the great festivals of the Jewish faith (Passover, Tabernacles, the Feast of Lights). These are solemn religious ceremonies, to be sure, but also celebrations, occasion for rejoicing—religious parties, if you will. Jesus, according to John, made it a point to attend these feasts and celebrate them. Besides all of this, John's Gospel constantly refers to food and drink—the bread of life, for example, or living water. Jesus likened himself to a vine and the disciples to branches of that vine—meaning, of course, that his purpose is to bring forth the fruit of the vine, good wine.

All of this is to say that the remarkable insistence on celebration in John means that this last chapter—as the account of a party—is not so distant from or foreign to the rest of the Gospel as it at first seems. So, our initial impression of strangeness about this chapter recedes somewhat. We must admit the possibility that there are real, genuine links between John 21 and the first twenty chapters of the Fourth Gospel.

IV

Well, if this is a party, what kind of party is it? Literally, it's a picnic at the beach; it's a fish fry with freshly baked bread on the side. (Again, I'm guessing when I say that the bread was fresh; the text doesn't say that. But remember that Jesus' wine at the wedding in Cana was the very best available, and we all know that bread is best when it's hot out of the oven. Since Jesus is responsible for this, I feel certain it would have taken first prize in any bake-off.) And now, as with everything else in John's Gospel, this simple story begins to take on theological meaning.

And the first theologically significant point is that this party is a post-Resurrection party. It's a celebration that occurs in the aftermath (and afterglow) of the Resurrection. The disciples had had many parties with Jesus before this one, all of which had contained levels of meaning none of them had fully understood. But this one was the most significant of all because it came in the wake of the most significant thing yet about Jesus—namely, that God had raised him from the dead. The disciples had put their faith in Jesus; the Crucifixion had shattered that faith, seeming to give the lie to all they had believed. The Crucifixion had apparently destroyed everything that had given meaning and purpose and significance to their lives. And it must have been especially bitter to Peter, the focal point of Chapter 21, because it was the occasion of his denial of Jesus. The Crucifixion seemed to be the end of all their hopes and dreams.

But it wasn't. The one thing they believed couldn't happen had happened. The tomb was empty, Jesus' body was gone, and Jesus himself began appearing to them. And they believed. This time there could be no doubt, no uncertainty. Jesus was what he had claimed to be, the Messiah, the Son of God, the Savior. "Jesus Christ, Son of God, Savior" was an early acronym composed of the first letters of each of those words. When these Greek letters are put together, they spell the word *ichthus*, "fish." Jesus on the shore of Galilee offered the disciples fish to eat; that is, he offered them himself. He was alive, not dead. And his life gives life to all who believe in him, all who accept his offer of spiritual food. This fish fry was more than just a meal satisfying physical hunger. It was a post-Resurrection meal of communion with the

Risen Lord, who is the Bread of Life, who is *ichthus*, Jesus Christ, Son of God, Savior.

V

But saying that this meal is to be understood in the light of the Resurrection says only half of what needs to be said, because the Resurrection is not itself the end of God's redemptive activity. Rather, it is merely the turning point or the climax of salvation history. It is the point on which history turns, when good finally gets the upper hand over evil, and we know that good will eventually triumph. But we need to stress the word *eventually*. The end, the *eschaton*, has not yet come. So, there is still work to be done, there are ministries to be performed, there are sheep to be fed.

This is why Jesus called Peter aside to walk with him along the shore of Galilee, apart from the other disciples, and asked him, "Do you love me, really love me?" And Peter, who must have been suffering terribly as he remembered his denials, said, "Yes, Lord, you know I love you." "Well," Jesus said, "feed my sheep; take care of my flock." Three time Jesus gently asked this painful question, and three times Peter asserted his love, and three times Jesus commanded Peter to "feed my sheep." Jesus was telling Peter that the Resurrection wasn't the end of his discipleship, but rather the beginning. Peter and all of Jesus' disciples were to celebrate the Resurrection. But they were also to get about the task that needed to be done between the Resurrection and Jesus' ultimate return. It is a post-Resurrection party, but it is also a pre-eschatological party as well.

And what about us? What does the post-Resurrection, pre-eschatological fish fry and bake-off mean to us? It means everything, because the party that started 2,000 years ago on the shore of the Sea of Galilee is still in progress. In fact, we're at the party right now, this very moment. We have been invited to this Supper of the Lamb and have R.S.V.P.'d that we gladly accept. It is our acceptance of this invitation that makes us Christians. People who aren't Christians are people who either haven't heard about the party or who have refused to join in. We are Christians because we have said yes to the invitation to the best party ever thrown by anyone, anywhere.

Everyone and everything have been invited. Our host is the Lord of Life, who conquered death, whose Resurrection was no mere fish story. The Resurrection stories grew bigger with each telling, not because the disciples got more inventive with their lying, but because no single story could ever begin to contain the reality this story pointed to. If we believe this, the ultimate fish story, if we say yes to the invitation to this post-Resurrection, pre-eschatological celebration, then the Lord of Life, who conquered death and is our host, will begin to live in us and nourish our souls with eternal food.

The Little Cross of Horrors

Matthew 27:15-46

I

In what proves to be, in more ways than one, her finale in the movie *The Little Shop of Horrors*, Audrey II, the people-eating plant bent on world conquest, sings: "I'm a mean, green mother from outer space, and I'm mad." This initial obscenity is followed by a string of obscenities aimed at the only person who knows her real intentions and, therefore, the only person who can stop her. This is Seymour Krellborn, the nerdish, wimpy clerk of the little shop, who found Audrey II and nursed her to life—literally giving his blood that she might live. Seymour has aided and abetted, albeit unwittingly, Audrey II's quest for power. But by the end of the movie, he realizes what she is up to, and in the best tradition of Hollywood heroes, he stands up to her and declares, "Only one of us will come out of this alive!" Audrey II just laughs her obscene laugh and then proceeds to bring the shop down quite literally on Seymour, who is buried in the rubble.

Seymour's challenge to Audrey II is foolish and quixotic. She has the power, guile, and intelligence. All Seymour has is his own innate goodness and his determination to stop her at all cost. "I'm a mean, green mother from outer space, and I'm mad. I'm a mean, green mother from outer space, and it looks like you've been had," Audrey II sings. Indeed, it does look as if Seymour has had it. But at the very moment of Audrey II's triumph, the tables are turned. Seymour reaches up through the rubble, finds a high-voltage line that Audrey II severed in trashing the shop, and applies its live end to one of her many tentacles. "Oh, wow!" she exclaims, experiencing both literally

37

and figuratively the shock of her life. (She actually says something much stronger, but I can't reproduce that here.)

This electrifying experience is also illuminating. She realizes, just before exploding into thousands of harmless sparks, into nothingness, that her destructive glee in trashing the shop has made her own destruction possible. Seymour emerges from the rubble—battered, bruised, bloody, but unbowed—and goes to the arms of his true love, the original Audrey after whom he had named this evil plant. The two of them go off into the sunset to start their life anew in their picture-perfect, Better-Homes-and-Gardens house in the mythical land of "Somewhere That's Green."

II

The Little Shop of Horrors is intended as entertainment and social satire and nothing more. Nevertheless, I think this movie has a theological dimension, intended or not, because the character of Audrey II is an almost perfect portrait of evil. She is an obscene character, as foul-mouthed an antagonist as we'll ever see in a movie. But her obscenity is not what makes her evil. Rather, her evil character is what makes her obscene. And what makes her character evil is her joy in pointless destruction. Destructiveness is her dominant personality trait. She enjoys trashing the shop and taunting Seymour. And what she does in this microcosm is what she intends for the world. Whatever else evil is and whatever else evil does, its intention and result are always destruction.

Ultimately, of course, evil's destruction is self-destruction. But if misery loves company, so does evil. The destructiveness of evil always expands to include others, who are themselves in most cases innocent. A drunk man gets behind the wheel of his car and then slams into another car, killing a family. If the accident doesn't kill the drunk, then the alcohol eventually will. But in the meantime, a family whose only crime was being in the wrong place at the wrong time is destroyed. A person hooked on drugs destroys his or her life, it's true. But it's also true that addicts try to involve others in their addiction. Evil is tragic because it is social. Its destructiveness reaches out to encompass as many people as possible.

The destructiveness of evil is also ultimately pointless. There is no pleasure evil can give that we cannot have in some licit form. The Bible inveighs against the misuse of alcohol, not its use. It is the adulteration of sex the Bible condemns, not sex itself. The high of a drug experience cannot be qualitatively superior to the experience of God in worship. (Many students of mystical experience have commented on the parallels between drug-induced ecstasy and mystical communion with God. The difference is that drugs addict, enslave, and destroy; while the experience of worship gives life.) Whatever pleasure evil gives in the short run is in the long run pointless, because the pleasure could have been experienced in some other, legitimate way.

III

The real destructive power of evil, however, does not lie in its capacity for physical destruction. Rather, its destructiveness is in its power to corrupt the soul, the inner reality that makes us human. The physical destruction Audrey II visits on Orin Scrivello, Mr. Mushnik, and the little shop merely symbolizes the inner destruction already in progress. Scrivello, the sadistic dentist, has already gone far down the road of spiritual destruction when Audrey II appears to hasten the process. Like Audrey II, his destruction comes at his own hand, the result of one of his perverted pleasures. Mr. Mushnik, owner of the little shop, was spiritually destroyed before Audrey II ever made a meal of him. Basically a good man with good impulses, he nevertheless succumbs to the temptation of greed, thinking that he can get rid of Seymour and keep all the profits of the shop for himself. His spiritual destruction is what leads to his physical destruction.

We see the spiritual destructiveness of evil in the wasted faces of the people who live "Downtown" on skid row. They are homeless, hopeless, and helpless. When Mr. Mushnik chases Crystal, Ronette, and Chiffon (the Greek chorus of this movie) from the front of his shop, he yells at them, "How are you going to better yourselves?" And Crystal, Ronette, and Chiffon answer, "Mister, when you're from skid row, there ain't no such thing." The devastation, wastefulness, and destruction of a skid row is really the devastation, wastefulness, and destruction of the human spirit.

Part of the spiritual destructiveness of evil is its ever-diminishing returns. The pleasures of evil are at first sweet. At first, their price is well within our ability to pay. But that doesn't last long. Audrey II's first words are when she whines, "Feed me!" "Feed me!" And Seymour is naturally shocked at hearing a talking plant. But he should have been more shocked at the sinister implications these words carry. "Feed me!" is the first and unceasing cry of evil. "Feed me, and I'll give you what you want" is the promise evil makes. At first, evil delivers on its promises—the shop becomes financially successful, Seymour gets the girl of his dreams. However, while these successes grow, so do Audrey II and her appetites. In each scene, she's bigger, stronger, more powerful, and hungrier. Drops of blood from Seymour's bandaged fingers quickly become insufficient, and she begins demanding more.

"Feed me!" evil demands. But its feeding is a parody of nourishment. Its appetites can never be satisfied. Its demands are for ever-greater sacrifices of time, resources, and relationships, while giving less and less in return. Once the appetites of evil take root in us, they won't be satisfied, and we will be consumed.

IV

For a Christian, the single most evil act of human history, the single event that causes the greatest horror, is the crucifixion of Christ. The evil of an Audrey II is nothing but a pale fictional image of the very real evil of the cross. For a Christian, not even the evil of the great criminals of history—the Caligulas, the Neros, the Attilas, the Hitlers, the Charles Mansons—can compare to the evil and horror of the cross. Non-Christians will probably take exception and object that what Hitler did was far worse than the death of Jesus, terrible as that may have been. Isn't the death of six million Jews six million times more horrible than the death of Jesus?

I admit the force of this objection but maintain that for a Christian the Crucifixion is the most evil and horrible event of history. Why? What is it about the Crucifixion that makes it so horrible? Why is the cross a cross of horrors? The road down which the answer to this question lies is not an easy one to follow. There are many side paths that falsely appear to be the main thoroughfare. And some of these can lead to disastrous destinations—the best known being that of anti-Semitism, the charge that the Jews killed Jesus because they were purely evil men, totally given over to Satan's service. This is a road that leads to a precipice. Once we start down it, our momentum can become so great that it impels us over the edge to destruction below. To take the road of blaming the Jews as Christ-killers is to succumb to evil and suffer the horrors of spiritual destruction.

Other roads are dead ends, such as the road that leads to the conclusion that the Crucifixion is so evil because Jesus was innocent. That, in itself, hardly justifies this claim because the legalized death of innocent victims happens time and time again on a far greater scale than the cross. Besides, in one sense I'm not sure Jesus was innocent. The religious and political authorities who put Jesus to death saw very clearly that Jesus was a threat— to their power, status, and authority, of course, but also to the very delicate, fragile relationship existing between Rome and the Jewish people. The upsetting of this relationship could have brought on a political disaster in which many, many innocent people would suffer and die (as in fact happened forty years later when Roman armies destroyed Jerusalem and the Jews effectively ceased to be a nation). The destruction of the Jewish state in A.D. 70 was one of the great tragedies of human history, which continues to have incalculable impact. The Jewish leaders who authorized Jesus' death saw very clearly that Jesus had the potential to so revolutionize relations with Rome that it was indeed better from their perspective "that one man should die for the people, than that the whole nation should be destroyed." (John 11:50)

V

The evil of the cross does not lie in the suffering of Christ, as terrible as that was. The evil of the cross does not lie in the intentions of the ones who put Jesus to death. At the very worst, their motives were mixed. They were no more evil than you or I. So, we ask again: Why is the cross a cross of horrors? Why is it the most evil event in history? For a Christian, the answer lies in what this event means. The Crucifixion is the act by which the human race said no to the final, ultimate, complete revelation of God's love. It is the rejection of the only one who can save us from all hurtful and destructive things, especially the things that would destroy the spirit. It is the turning of our backs on the only one who can give us life, peace, and joy. It is our spurning of the only one who can save us from sin and sin's consequence, death. There can be no fuller revelation of God's love to us than this, and in the Crucifixion we said that we didn't want to have anything to do with that love.

Matthew's account of the Crucifixion is full of the horror of this event. There's the substitution of the criminal Barabbas for the innocent Jesus. There's the crowd whipped into a frenzy so that they shout down all of Pilate's attempts to be reasonable. There's Pilate's attempt to absolve himself of responsibility by washing his hands and the crowd's chilling clamor for the responsibility to be on them and their children. There's the physical abuse the soldiers inflict on Jesus and the mental anguish that mockery must have caused him. There's the casual gambling at the foot of the cross while Jesus dies and the ironic inscription placed over Jesus' head. There's the identification of Jesus with bandits and the verbal taunts of the crowd. Worst of all, there's that awful cry, "My God, my God, why has Thou forsaken me?"—which may indeed mean that Jesus was quoting Psalm 22, but which is awful nonetheless.

However, the most chilling words in all of Matthew's account are in verse 19, an incident that appears to have been added later almost as an afterthought. The wife of Pilate sends her husband an urgent and ominous message. She tells Pilate that she has "suffered a great deal in a dream" because of Jesus. So, she says, "Have nothing to do with that innocent man." Some people read this advice as the voice of conscience and as a warning from God. Perhaps it is. She does say that Jesus is innocent. Nevertheless, her real motivation seems to be fear. She has had a nightmare about Jesus, and she is scared. That Jesus is innocent seems to be less important than that his innocence causes her to suffer.

Have nothing to do with Jesus. The cross is horrible because through it we said no to the love of God, which alone can save us. To reject this love is to start down the path of pointless spiritual destruction. That is why the cross is a cross of horrors.

A Fine Cold Morning in a Brand New Age

Matthew 28:1-10

I

One of my earliest memories is an Easter Sunday morning when I was almost four years old. What I remember is standing in front of our house with my two sisters, waiting, I suppose, for my parents to come out and take us to church. We were all dressed up in our new Easter clothes. The sky was very blue, and the clouds were very white against that blue sky. It was one of those spring mornings that are fresh and new, the whole world coming alive with new life. But the thing I remember most clearly about this particular day is that it was Easter. I know it was Easter because I remember looking up in the sky thinking that I would see Jesus returning in the clouds. Somehow I had gotten the notion, not yet being four years old, that Easter Sunday was the day Jesus came back. I had also gotten the notion that Jesus would be coming in the sky, and I would be able to see him if I looked up. All of this was prompted, probably, by something one of my sisters had said about its being Easter Sunday, though I have no idea what that might have been. In my childish way I knew that Easter had something to do with Jesus coming back to us, with Jesus being present with us.

This is not my earliest memory, but it is my earliest memory of anything religious. I mention it because, in a way, it is ironic that this expectation that Jesus would come on Easter Sunday was my introduction to the Christian faith. I say it is ironic because my subsequent religious upbringing hardly stressed the Resurrection at all. The kind of theology I grew up on is what I call "Crucifixion Theology" or a "Theology of the Cross." Whatever else I may have been taught about the Christian faith, it always came back and was subordinate to the single most important thing—that Jesus died a horrible death for us on the cross. This theology permeated the sermons I heard and the songs we sang in our services—sermons about the blood of Jesus, the Lamb of God slain for our sins, the Substitutionary Atonement, and songs with titles like "The Old Rugged Cross," "Washed in the Blood of the Lamb," and "There Is a Fountain Filled with Blood." It wasn't that preachers never preached on any other subject or that we never sang anything but songs about the death of Jesus. Rather, it was that everything else was subordinate to this one event. If anyone ever asked, "What is it that saves us?" the immediate answer was, "The death of Jesus on the cross."

II

Quite clearly this is a true statement for a Christian—it is Jesus' death that saves us. The problem is that while what this affirms is true, it only affirms part of the truth. This Crucifixion theology is partial and incomplete; and because it is a one-sided presentation of the gospel, it is susceptible to misunderstanding and extremes. One such misunderstanding is a theory of the Atonement called the Substitutionary Atonement. It goes something like this:

God is a just and loving God, but above all a *just* God, who at all times demands justice. If one of God's laws is broken, the offender must pay the penalty for the offense or else God's justice is not satisfied. The metaphor that rules this theory of Atonement is that of the law court, in which guilty parties are brought before a judge who pronounces sentence. The sentence for each offense is prescribed by law, and there can be no escaping the penalty. The law court, in this metaphor, can only hand out mandatory sentences. The judge is God. The offenders, the lawbreakers, are you and I and the whole human race. Our offense is sin, and the mandatory sentence for this sin is death, complete and everlasting separation from God in hell. God's mercy and love would like to suspend the death sentence, but God's justice would not thereby be satisfied. (Remember that, above all else, God is a God of justice.) Therefore, you and I must die for our sins. This sentence of death is irrevocable.

Clearly, such a situation is intolerable. How can God let the whole human race be lost? Well, if a substitute could be found to die in our stead, God's justice would be satisfied (because the death sentence had been carried out), but so would God's mercy and love (because God wouldn't lose the human race). Is it possible to find such a substitute? Remember that the substitute must cover *all* the sins of *all* of us. The substitute's goodness must, therefore, be infinite and perfect goodness, or otherwise the substitute would, like the rest of us, deserve to die. Enter Jesus. He volunteers to become incarnate as a human being while remaining free of sin.

His death would, therefore, be an acceptable substitute. Furthermore, since Jesus is the Second Person of the Godhead, his goodness will have the requisite infinitude and perfection and be sufficient to cover all of the sins of all of us. God agrees to this plan and sends Jesus into the world for the sole purpose of dying (sort of like a divine Kamikaze pilot); and when Jesus does finally die, God the judge will no longer condemn anyone who accepts this substitute.

For some people this theory is the only way to understand the Atonement, and for many others it is the primary way. It's the theory I grew up on. Nevertheless, there was another theory of Atonement, which was sometimes presented as a supplement to the first. It's called the Ransom Theory and goes something like this: When God threw Satan out of heaven for disobedience, Satan decided to get back at God by capturing some of God's territory. Satan was particularly interested in getting the human race, since we were the special purpose of creation. He took the form of a snake and tempted Eve, who obligingly yielded and also got Adam to yield too. Through Adam and Eve every subsequent human being was tainted with sin, and so the whole human race was taken captive by Satan. Satan's purpose was to hold us for ransom and make God pay a dear price. Once again, the situation is intolerable; something must be done. But what? Satan presents God with a breathtaking, utterly outrageous proposition. Satan will exchange the human race for the Son of God, the Second Person of the Trinity. God agrees. Jesus the Incarnate Son of God willingly places himself totally within Satan's destructive power and suffers death on the cross. Jesus is taken hostage in the Crucifixion, and we are set free.

God, however, had a trump card, an ace up the divine sleeve.

Satan had been playing with a stacked deck and loaded dice and didn't know it. God's trump card is the Resurrection. On the third day, God raises Jesus from the dead, and Satan (that old fool) finds out too late that he has been fooled. He loses both the human race and Jesus. He has no more hostages to ransom.

III

These theories have undoubtedly helped some Christians understand the saving power of Christ, but for me they were never very convincing. The Substitutionary Atonement is fatally flawed by an inconsistency. On the one hand, it insists that God is above all else a just God, but then it asserts on the other hand that God will allow a totally innocent person to die in the place of others. If anything is an injustice, it is punishing an innocent person for someone else's crimes. Surely, justice demands that I suffer for my sins and you suffer for yours. How could Christ's substitution satisfy God's justice, when such an act is so grossly unjust?

And the Ransom Theory fares no better. What it really says is that we should understand God as a high-stakes poker player who cheats. God makes a deal with Satan but all the time has a stacked deck, marked cards, loaded dice weighted so that divine, not diabolical, numbers come up every time.

The real problem with both theories is that neither really takes the Resurrection seriously. They both make a fundamental mistake of separating the meaning of the Crucifixion from the meaning of the Resurrection and then assuming that the Crucifixion is what is really important. The Resurrection becomes sort of an adjunct to the main event, tacked on to prove that Jesus really was God (in case you missed it). And though the Resurrection is necessary in the Ransom Theory (notice that it saves Jesus from hell), the Crucifixion without the Resurrection has already saved you and me. The New Testament affirms that it is everything about Jesus that saves us—his life, death, and resurrection—all taken together as one single act of salvation. But the Ransom Theory separates Crucifixion from Resurrection and has the one save *us* and the other save *Jesus*.

The truth is that we must never separate the cross of Christ from the Resurrection of Christ, because if we do, we take away Christ's saving power. Without the Resurrection, the cross becomes nothing more than simply another example of the gross cruelty and injustice of the world. Another good man gets killed. So what? That's the end of the story; it happens every day; there's no news in that. Crucifixion loses its power without Resurrection. And Resurrection without Crucifixion is simply an inexplicable, strange, marvelous event with no meaning. That someone rose from the dead in itself does nothing to save us. What saves us is that it was Jesus who rose from the dead; it was the Crucified One who returned to life.

So, what is it about the Resurrection that makes it the necessary complement to the Crucifixion? What does the Resurrection mean, so that without it the Crucifixion becomes nothing but one more hideous, horrible crime?

IV

No one has better expressed in a popular way the meaning of the Resurrection than Darrell Adams, a contemporary gospel music artist. In his album, *Home*, he has two songs about the Resurrection that capture its meaning. The first is called "A Fine Cold Morning" and goes like this:[1]

> *They nailed him to a tree that was rough and tall.*
> *He died on a day dark and gray.*
> *They put him in the ground thinking that was all.*
> *Jesus rolled the stone away.*
>
> *They laid him in a tomb that was rocky and deep,*
> *With guards around it night and day.*
> *But when the Spirit comes saying "Rise from your sleep,"*
> *Jesus rolled the stone away.*
>
> *On a fine, fine cold morning,*
> *On a fine, fine cold day,*
> *It was early in the morning come Easter-rise,*
> *Jesus rolled the stone away.*

The first thing to notice is that from a human point of view the cross is final. "They put him in the ground thinking that was all." To kill Christ is to utterly reject God and what God is doing for our salvation. The Crucifixion is the end as far as we're concerned. We want to be certain that it is the end, so we put our guards up just to make sure. From our point of view the Crucifixion is final, but not from God's point of view. God reverses all that we have done, and Jesus rolls the stone away when the Spirit comes. Those guards we posted couldn't stop it, once the Spirit spoke. And so, our judgment that it's all over gets turned upside down, and God says through the act of the Resurrection, "No, it's only just begun."

That is why Easter Sunday morning is both fine and cold. It's a fine morning because we would quite literally be in one hell of a mess had God not raised Jesus from the dead. Death would be the end, and we would have no hope beyond our mundane existence. The Resurrection, however, says that life is the final word about us, not death. That's a fine word, a good word to hear. But why a *cold* morning? Why not a warm morning, with gentle breezes and the sweet songs of birds? Because coldness is the sensation of reality. Investors hope to reap cold, hard cash. Investigators deal only in the cold, hard facts. Poets write chillingly of the "cold embrace of death." What wakes you up in the morning, what brings you back to reality better than the splash of cold water in your face? Easter was a cold morning because the greatest reality of all became real in that event—the reality that the life of God is stronger than the destructiveness of evil.

There's more. Easter is an ending, the end of our attempts to put God off, of telling God to go away and leave us alone. But it is also a beginning—the beginning of a brand new age.[2]

It once was an age of violence.
The whole world lived in fear
Of one who held a gun or knife
Or sword or bomb or spear.

And when they nailed up Jesus,
The army did the chore.
But come next Sunday morning,
The weapons lost the war.

It once was an age of government.
Everybody knew
The one who had the palace and the crown
Had all the aces too.
And the Cross that Jesus died on
Was mighty Caesar's thing.
But come next Sunday morning,
There's a whole new kind of king!

It once was an age of sin and death.
The hissing snake of pride

Was wrapped around the earth so tight
It seemed all good had died.
And when they strung up Jesus,
The venom killed him dead.
But come next Sunday morning,
He crushed the serpent's head.

And it's a brand new age we're living in.
The Kingdom's breaking in my friends
And it's already here.
There's nothing left in guns or kings
Or even death to fear.
So live the Good News unafraid.
Shout the difference Easter made.
Citizens of God's new age —
God has overcome.
We shall overcome.

The resurrection of Christ was the beginning of a new age in human history, an age in which all the old standards and old ways of doing things are overturned. In the old way of doing things violence and power and the threat of death hold sway. We cower in fear before their power and fall helpless and hopeless. The old way of doing things seems utterly triumphant at first because it succeeds in nailing Jesus up, killing the very Son of God. But God answers this human rejection of divine love with a divine rejection of human hate and evil. Violence, power, and death are not the final words. The final word is the Resurrection. The final word is a life that no tomb could ever contain.

"The Kingdom's coming in my friends, and it's already here." The power of God is here and now, and you and I can be a part of it. The consequence of a kingdom that comes with a cross is this brand new age. It's a new way of living that transcends our old ways; it's the kingdom of Good News that we live. It's a story we tell of the difference Easter makes. And what an incredible story that is. It's the story that there's nothing left to fear—not even the most fearsome of all realities, death. Not even death has any power over us any more because the Resurrection broke the power of death once and for all.

V

There is a sense in which after the Crucifixion God does leave us alone. We've chosen rejection, and God respects our free choice. We may choose not to believe in the Resurrection. And if we do, we remain under the power and threat of death. The old ways of doing things still exert their fearsome power over us. Each of us individually must decide whether or not to believe this incredible story. And God won't overrule our decisions.

But there's another sense in which it is impossible for God to leave us alone. The very nature of God is life. God's reality gives life to everything else. And insofar as we have any reality at all, we touch God's reality, life itself. To kill Jesus cannot be the final reality because "God was in Christ reconciling the world to himself." *God* was in Christ, and that means that Jesus could not remain dead. We may continue to reject God, but God will never cease coming to us with the offer of life. Death can never be the final word about God, and it can never be the final word about Jesus. The very worst we can do, crucify Christ, cannot get rid of God.

In the Crucifixion, we say: Let the old age of sin and death continue. In the Resurrection, God says: Let the brand new age of life and love begin.

In the Crucifixion, we reject Christ and say: Leave us alone! In the Resurrection, God rejects our rejection and says: I'll never leave you alone. You can't kill me or my love for you. I'll always be coming back again.

In the Crucifixion, we say no to God. In the Resurrection, God says no to our no; God says yes to us.

Every day there's the possibility that we can turn our rejection into acceptance, our no into yes, our act of crucifixion into God's act of resurrection. This is good news worth shouting about; this a gospel worth living. Christ is risen. And we no longer need to fear even death itself.

Notes

1. "Fine Cold Morning" (c) 1986 Windmill Power Music, ASCAP. Lyric by Richard Vinson from the album *HOME* by Darrell Adams. Contact: Windmill Power Music, P.O. Box 7964, Louisville, KY 40257.

2. "Brand New Age" (c) 1986 Windmill Power Music, ASCAP. Lyric by Paul D. Duke from the album *HOME* by Darrell Adams. Contact: Windmill Power Music, P.O. Box 7964, Louisville, KY 40257.

Contemporary Culture

Grace and Responsibility for Creation

Luke 15:11-32

I

Perhaps nothing—not even sex—is a touchier subject for Christians, or one more liable to misunderstanding, than the subject of money. Each fall, local congregations gear themselves up for their stewardship drives, with the tacit understanding that everyone involved would really rather be doing something else. And everyone—from the ministers on down—breathes a sigh of relief when the campaign is finally over and the budget is subscribed. The final subscription doesn't even have to be 100 percent. If the congregation has come close to the desired goal, all seem satisfied and try to put the issue behind them for another year.

Why the giving of money should cause undue anxiety in ministers and congregations alike is, in some ways, difficult to explain. Jesus, after all, told his disciples not to worry overmuch about such things. God would take care of them in much the same way God takes care of the birds of the air and the flowers of the field. Nevertheless, stewardship campaigns cause anxieties. Perhaps Christians in rich congregations feel a vague sense of guilt about having money, and stewardship campaigns simply remind them of their wealth (about which they do worry, in spite of Jesus' injunction). Furthermore, they remember that Jesus was a poor man who had virtually no material resources of his own and that he told the rich young ruler to sell everything in order to be a disciple. They also remember that the rich young ruler simply couldn't do what Jesus asked (not even for the sake of the kingdom) and that Jesus then made a disturbing comment about rich people and camels and the eye of a needle.

As for members of poor congregations, they may resent being asked to give up some of the money they *do* have, which is little enough to begin with.

So, whether rich or poor, when the time for emphasizing stewardship comes around, Christians tend to get anxious and uncomfortable.

II

Let me suggest another reason why Christians may be touchy about the issue of money. Money makes the whole question of Christian discipleship more difficult and confusing than it already is. Christianity proclaims the free grace of God available to all through Jesus Christ with no strings attached. None of us can earn this grace by doing good deeds; none of us deserves this grace by virtue of an inherently good nature; and none of us can buy this grace at any price, no matter how wealthy we may be. Yet, the temptation arises in every generation of Christians to try to do something to earn what can only be freely given and received. And what more obvious way to make us deserving—especially in our consumer society, where we tend to measure the worth of virtually everything in terms of money— than to give our possessions liberally to God.

As a result, we feel a tension between what we know the gospel is (God's undeserved grace toward us in Jesus) and the way we usually evaluate worth (in monetary terms). If the church really believed all it says about the undeservedness of grace, the free gift of salvation in Christ, then why all the emphasis on giving money and why all the sometimes not-so-subtle promise of blessing and prosperity for all who give enough? Grace is free. But are you really a good Christian if you don't give money to the church? Wouldn't it be a lot simpler if the Christian faith were just a straightforward business transaction in which for X amount of money we would receive an appropriate place in the kingdom (rather like buying a pew at church)?

And that's not all. Grace somehow grates on us, rubs us the wrong way. How can anything as valuable as our salvation be free? We're so accustomed to paying for what we want that we feel just a little bit resentful that God wants to save us without requiring a single blessed thing from us. It sounds too good to be true. It sounds for all the world like a con job or a scam. The Better Business Bureau is always warning us to be suspicious of deals like that. Furthermore, accepting grace is an implicit admission of our own unworthiness to receive it and our own inability to save ourselves. Who wants to admit need and weakness in this brave new world of "standing tall" and saving ourselves by new improved missiles, tanks, and bombers?

III

We seem to have gotten ourselves into an unfair double-bind. On the one hand, we want to be disciples of the one who taught his disciples not to worry about material things. On the other hand, that discipleship seems to involve us necessarily in the use of material things. After all, how can we worship and teach the gospel without places for those activities to occur and supplies for them to occur with? How can we minister to people who are sick or homeless or outcast without establishing hospitals and orphanages and missions to do these ministries? How can we have a trained and effective ministerial leadership without paying for it?

It's true that ministry can and does and should occur in the course of our everyday lives as Christians. And it's also true that the church could get along without beautiful sanctuaries, magnificent pipe organs, and a trained clergy, if it absolutely had to. And it's true that such material institutions can easily become sources of powerful temptations and causes of stumbling. Anyone familiar with the history of the church knows how easily Christians can be led to focus on their institutions, forgetting very quickly the reasons for having them.

All of this is true. Nevertheless, we are material creatures living in a material world created by a God who proclaimed it all to be good. We depend on this material world for our existence. If we are to be ministers of Christ in this world, we will have to minister to every kind of need, just as Jesus did. He healed bodies as well as souls, fed physically hungry people as well as the spiritually hungry, and on one occasion even provided some very good wine for a party and saved the host from social humiliation. In other words, Jesus used material things to meet human need—even, surprisingly, the need to have a good time. So must we, if we are to be his disciples.

IV

The real problem isn't money. Money simply comes to stand for the deeper problem underlying our Christian anxieties. The real problem is that we are not entirely at ease with being material creatures in a material creation. We tend to think that our faith concerns only spiritual matters, and therefore we have a hard time connecting the spiritual with the material. We tend to divide our lives into neat compartments (the secular and the sacred) and think that their intersection is about as likely as the meeting of east and west. But for Christians there is a connection between these two aspects of our lives, and it's found in the doctrine of creation.

The Bible begins with the assertion that God created the world and that that creation was good. Implicit in the idea of creation was the idea of the world belonging to God. "The earth is the LORD's," the psalmist wrote, "and they that dwell therein." The idea of the physical universe belonging to God immediately raised an important issue—namely, by what right do we human beings use the world for our own purposes? The answer the Bible gave was a simple one. We rightfully use the world because God not only lets us but actually commands us to do so. "Let us make humankind in our image, according to our likeness; and let them have dominion over the fish of the sea, and over the birds of the air, and over the cattle, and over all the earth," the author of Genesis 1 wrote.

It is easy to misunderstand this verse as giving us carte blanche to do whatever we want with the created order. But that is a misunderstanding. Our dominion over the earth is not quite that simple because along with the privilege of using God's creation, we were also given the corresponding responsibility of respecting it as God's creation. The doctrine of Creation implies a corresponding doctrine of stewardship. We human beings are created to be stewards of God's possession, the good earth. And if we are to be stewards, then we are also to be accountable for what we do with the earth—that is, with all material things.

In other words, one of the ways the Bible defines human nature is in terms of stewardship. The human creation is that part of creation responsible for the well-being of the rest of creation. And all of it belongs to God. This, indeed, is the primary meaning of the idea of stewardship—responsible use of and care for another's material possessions.

V

Once again, we need to guard against misunderstanding. Responsibility for creation seems to involve obligations, duties that we must perform. But once we begin thinking of responsibility in terms of obligation or duty, we have introduced a foreign element into our stewardship of God's resources. An obligation is something imposed on us from without. Someone does us a favor, and we're "much obliged" to them. A responsibility, in contrast, is something we choose to do because of an inward response to some outer reality. (*Response* and *responsibility* are more than just etymologically related.) Let me illustrate the difference between an obligation and a responsibility.

Most parents, more or less, provide for the needs of their children. For some parents this is an obligation, while for others it is a responsibility. Various sorts of external pressures motivate the first sort of parent—fear of social disapproval or legal problems, for example, if they don't provide. The second sort of parent has a different motivation—the internal desire to give their children what is best for them. This internal desire arises out of their response of love to that child's existence. Parents who see their children as responsibilities are responding to the reality of their children—realities the parents themselves created out of another loving response to another reality, the response of love to each other. Parents who are responsible for their children out of a loving response provide for their children because they want to, not because they have to. They give their children everything they can that's needful, willingly and without begrudging the cost or sacrifice.

In the parable of the prodigal son, the father acts precisely in this responsible way. (Perhaps we should call this the parable of the responsible parent.) The prodigal's need upon returning home is to realize he has been accepted back. The father—out of a deep love for his son that no amount of debauchery could ever destroy—responds to this need and throws a party that says "welcome home!" This story completely overthrows our usual understanding of responsibility. Most of us, I think, secretly question the father's response. Is this a responsible way to act?

Shouldn't the son be punished? At the least, shouldn't he be put on probation? Isn't the father really irresponsible for condoning irresponsible behavior? We may not voice these thoughts (since this story is Jesus'), but the older brother does speak our reservations and lets the father know them in no uncertain terms. The older brother, however, looks on life in terms of obligations, while the father looks on life in terms of responsibilities.

The Bible teaches us to be responsible to God—that is, to respond to what God has done for us in Christ. Christ shows us that God is loving and caring and ready to go to inordinate lengths to put right the things we've made wrong. Christ puts a human face on God, and that face is the face of unconditional, self-giving love. Christ gives us God's reality—not a new Law and not a new set of rules and regulations. And to those who accept this gift of God's reality, life will never be the same again. Christ transforms the whole basis for action and thought and feeling. The new basis for a Christian is love. "We love, because God first loved us," First John says.

And that transformation of life applies to what we normally call "stewardship," the way we use our money. The Christian life is a response of love to God's act of love in Christ. Our Christian giving of money, therefore, has no external requirement attached to it, as if the church were a tax collector who assessed Christian giving like the government assesses taxes. Instead, our giving comes from the inward response of love to love. God created the world, and the world belongs to God. God created us to be good stewards of that world. Our stewardship should come from our response of love to God's act of love.

Why, then, be anxious about what we give? Let us give joyfully and willingly and, as Paul put it, "cheerfully." We have freely received of God's grace. Let us freely give in response.

Soul-Searching and the New Year*

2 Corinthians 5:17; Revelation 21:1,5

I

The time of year now coming to a close—Advent, Christmas, New Year's—is a time paradoxical in its demands on us. On the one hand, the end of this holiday season is traditionally a time when we reflect on our lives and try to evaluate where we are and where we're going—a process that usually ends with resolutions to do better. On the other hand, this season is so full of activity and busyness that by the time we get to New Year's Day we may be so tired that the last thing we want to do is engage in a bit of soul-searching. We've been busy shopping, addressing and mailing Christmas cards, attending parties and special church services. Then, January 1 comes along with a further demand on our already depleted energies, whispering in our ears, "And what resolutions are you going to make today?"

It's not that we have nothing to make resolutions about. If any season (other than Lent) is likely to make us aware of the faults we should resolve to correct, it is this one. For one thing, our celebration of the birth of Christ ought to heighten our awareness of why God had to become incarnate in a human life. The Word made flesh was necessary because of the mess we have made of things. Even if we aren't guilty of the sins we ordinarily think of as the "big" ones—murder and adultery—nevertheless we all know those "little" sins we're all guilty of are enough to keep us from God. (Not that our sins matter all that much to God. Not

*For Dr. Tony Duncan, who told me I really ought to read *The Hitchhiker's Guide to the Galaxy.*

that, as far as God is concerned, they would be enough to keep us apart. Rather, they matter too much to us. We are of a divided mind, wanting God but wanting our sins as well. God simply wants us, sins and all, but we're too fastidious, saying in effect to God that we'll clean up our acts first. And that is really a way of saying we're not ready to give our sins up, since the surest way to get rid of a sin is to bring it to God. "Give me chastity and continence," St. Augustine prayed, "but not just now.")

For another thing, the very busyness of the season tends to bring out these faults, as the pace of our lives accelerates and we fret whether or not the gifts we give will be appreciated or whether or not we have sent all the cards we should or whether we've omitted anyone from our guest lists. At this time of year, we overeat, overdrink, overspend, don't get the rest we should— in short, we overindulge in every possible way. And the faults we normally keep in check in ordinary life are closer to the surface and quicker to express themselves. Do you ordinarily have a problem with impatience? alcohol? food? tobacco? finding time to be with your family? You can be sure that this holiday season will exacerbate these failings. So, when New Year's Day gets here, we're all aware of the faults we need to be working on.

II

Making resolutions about these faults is easy. It's the keeping of them that's hard. So, added to our already heightened sense of personal failings is the guilty awareness that no matter how hard we try, the bookies would lay substantial odds against our actually keeping a New Year's resolution. The whole business frustrates us. We know we ought to do better. We want to do better. We try; we really try. And we fail; we really fail. The upshot is that we are tempted to resolve not to make any more New Year's resolutions. And even that resolution fails as well; for when New Year's comes around again, we begin thinking, "I really ought to . . . ," and then the pattern repeats itself.

Adding to our frustration is the vague fear that self-reflection can actually be a mistake. If soul-searching goes very deep, it can show us things we might not rather see. And once we see something unfavorable about ourselves, we've lost the best answer we can give to excuse ourselves—"I didn't know I was that way." Once we've become aware of a previously hidden fault, we've got to do *something* about it. We can try to bury it again in our subconscious, or we can defiantly say "So what?" and resolve not to do anything about it. Or we can try to overcome it, in which case we're back at the impasse from which we tried to escape: resolutions are easy to make but hard to keep.

One of the characters in Douglas Adams' *Life, the Universe and Everything* illustrates the dangers of soul-searching. Zaphod Beeblebrox, the two-headed, three-armed president of the Galaxy, having done everything he ever thought he wanted to do (namely, hop around the galaxy having a good time in his wonderful spaceship *The Heart of Gold*), found himself alone in circumstances that created the ideal moment for some soul-searching, which, he concludes, had "clearly been an error," a shocking error. It was shocking, first, to discover that he actually had a soul, and second, that his soul was not "the totally wonderful object that he felt a man in his position had a natural right to expect."[1]

Like Zaphod Beeblebrox, most of us more or less assume we have a soul. Like him, we more or less assume our souls are pretty wonderful. And like him, we studiously ignore them if at all possible. When forced into some soul-searching, we, like him, experience the double shock of the actuality of the thing and its less than wonderful qualities. So, soul-searching is a dangerous and unpleasant activity we all try to avoid.

III

All of this is true. Nevertheless, we continue to be plagued by the vague suspicion that soul-searching is something we ought to do and that, if we were ever successful at it, we would be a lot happier. We vaguely suspect that soul-searching might actually turn out to be one of the most useful and rewarding things we could do, perhaps even satisfying. For one thing, as Aristotle pointed out, getting knowledge is a pleasurable activity. When that knowledge is self-knowledge, it is even more rewarding because it is knowledge of what is closest and most important to us—our own reality. We all know that getting knowledge can be difficult and at times painful. Nevertheless, the ultimate pleasure of discovering something we didn't know and wouldn't know had we not made the effort makes the pain and difficulty worthwhile.

Soul-searching can be rewarding.

It can also be useful. Socrates believed that "knowledge is virtue," by which he meant that knowing what is right means doing what is right. He was wrong about that, of course, as experience amply attests. Simply knowing the right doesn't guarantee that our practice will conform. But at least it is true that once we know a certain course of action is the right one, it becomes more difficult to act in a contrary manner. Self-knowledge can, therefore, be a good goad to right action.

It is useful in another way, as well. Self-reflection leading to greater self-knowledge produces a greater sense of self-integration. It is this sense of integration—of having all aspects of our lives in harmony with one another—that leads to integrity. And integrity is the bedrock that can keep us stable when everything else is shifting and changing. Integrity is the quality that enables us to cope with whatever life throws at us—curves, sinkers, even spitballs. Personal integrity doesn't guarantee that we will hit home runs every time. But it does guarantee that even if we strike out, we will have nothing to regret. The only thing that Satan couldn't take away from Job was his integrity. But integrity was enough to see Job through.

IV

All of this sounds good. It may even be true. But it also sounds esoteric, like something a fakir in India does on a bed of nails or a monk in Tibet does in reciting a mantra. Such exotic techniques may or may not produce self-knowledge. In any case, they are not what I am talking about. Zaphod Beeblebrox hadn't done anything strange when soul-searching caught up with him. In fact, he was going about his ordinary routine of looking for all the fun he could get when his unpleasant experience of soul-searching occurred. The self-reflection that leads to self-knowledge that leads to effective resolutions is something that occurs in the midst of life as we go about our daily affairs. It is our daily routine, in fact, that provides the data for our self-knowledge. The process of reflection on that data, or "soul-searching" as I have called it, is what Frederick Buechner calls "listening to your life."

In the second volume of his autobiography, *Now and Then*,

Buechner writes of a period of depression he experienced following a move to rural Vermont to devote all his time to writing. His novel wasn't going well, and his life had become a routine of seemingly trivial events, such as taking his children to school. It was a period of self-doubt for Buechner, reinforced by the national traumas of Vietnam, assassinations, and Watergate. Then Buechner received a request to deliver some lectures at Harvard on "religion and letters," and the word *letters* set off a train of thought that eventually led to a new perspective. The trivial events, as well as the traumatic, he now saw as letters in the literal sense of *A*'s and *B*'s and *C*'s out of which he was making the words of his life and the story those words composed. From this perspective, the very routine of life took on a new meaning. He could no longer see an event as trivial or merely routine because every event now had the potential to be a revelation. All events are the letters and words of our stories, and our stories are the ways we come to know ourselves and God.

> *. . . There is no event so commonplace but that God is present within it, always hiddenly, always leaving you room to recognize him or not to recognize him, but all the more fascinatingly because of that, all the more compellingly and hauntingly. In writing those [Harvard] lectures and the book they later turned into, it came to seem to me that if I were called upon to state in a few words the essence of everything I was trying to say both as a novelist and as a preacher, it would be something like this: Listen to your life. See it for the fathomless mystery that it is. In the boredom and pain of it no less than in the excitement and gladness: touch, taste, smell your way to the holy and hidden heart of it because in the last analysis all moments are key moments, and life itself is grace.*[2]

"Listen to your life. . . . All moments are key moments." This is something we all can do, every day, in almost any circumstance—to listen to what each event making up our daily lives says to us. All moments, no matter how mundane or seemingly trivial, can become the entrance to a new and more profound understanding of ourselves. What is this success telling me? What does this disappointment or failure say about who I am? If my days flow along in their ordinary course, what does the very ordinariness of my life say about God's grace to me?

V

As far back as we have historical records, the New Year has been a time of renewal and reflection and recommitment to basic values. There's nothing new about New Year's resolutions. But with Christ, something new has entered human history. It is the sanctifying of our earthly lives by the presence of Christ in them. "So if anyone is in Christ, there is a new creation," Paul wrote to the Corinthian Christians, "everything old has passed away; see, everything has become new!" (2 Corinthians 5:17). These are audacious words indeed, written to one of the most contentious, wrangling congregations in all of church history. The empirical evidence was against these words being true at Corinth. Nevertheless, it was to the Corinthian church that Paul wrote these words. Faith in Christ begins a process of renewal that's genuine, even in people like the Corinthians.

This is the promise of the Christian faith—power for the renewal of life, power (if you please) to keep your New Year's resolutions. But this Christian experience of renewal is not merely individual renewal—my new life or yours. Rather, what happens with each of us individually is simply a foretaste of what God has in store for the whole creation. And in fact, our personal, individual renewal is a part of that wider act of new creation that God is in the process of bringing about. It is fit that the Bible begins with the act of creation and ends with the promise of a new creation. "Then I saw a new heaven and a new earth; for the first heaven and the first earth had passed away," John the seer wrote. "And the one who was seated on the throne said, 'See, I am making all things new'" (Revelation 21:1,5).

Our attempts at renewal on New Year's Day with New Year's resolutions need not frustrate or intimidate us. We have confidence that renewal is possible because of the new life we've already experienced in Christ. It is not in our own power that we keep our resolutions to do better. It is, rather, in the power of Christ who is making all things—including us—new. This new life is happening in our lives through Christ. So, "listen to your life" this new year. It may just be the words of Christ you hear and the power of the new creation you experience.

Notes

1. Douglas Adams, *Life, the Universe, and Everything* (New York: Pocket Books, 1983), 68-69.

2. Frederick Buechner, *Now and Then* (New York: Harper & Row, Publishers, 1983), 87.

Stories, Our Stories, and The Story

Matthew 10:42

I

"Human supremacy may be the product of technology," Kathryn Morton writes in a *New York Times Book Review*, "but technology is, in turn, the product of man's fancy, the story of mankind is the story of Story itself."[1] We are human, she argues, because we tell stories—not because we have opposable thumbs, erect posture, or the ability to make tools, each of which we share with some nonhuman animal like chimpanzees. Morton then goes on to write:

> . . . *What got people out of the trees was something besides thumbs and gadgets. What did it, I am convinced, was a warp in the simian brain that made us insatiable for patterns—patterns of sequence, of behavior, of feeling— connections, reasons, causes: stories.*

> *We did not arise from the ape with a sharp rock, or even from the one who learned how to sharpen a dull rock, but from the one who saw the connection between sharpness of rock and soon-ness of supper. He pictured himself sitting down to eat and made the connection that now would be a good time to go gather some rocks from the stream down below, so they'd be ready when meat waddled by. . . . From the moment of that first muttered monologue, outlining the story of a better life through rock-gathering, to the moment of the moon landing was just a matter of steps. And each step was a story. . . .*[2]

We are human because we tell stories. And every activity characteristic of our humanity has to do in some way with storytelling—that is, with making a narrative pattern out of events. Children do this instinctively. Almost from the moment they can form sentences, they demand stories. "Daddy, tell me a story" is, of course, a way to delay bedtime. But it is also a reassurance to parents that their offspring are indeed human beings and not "noisy pet[s]," as Ms. Morton puts it. (We may in fact tell our pets stories, especially in moments of loneliness. But our pets don't request our stories, even if they do adopt attitudes of respectful, if uncomprehending, attention.) Children not only demand stories but also tell them themselves. We adults call it "play": cops and robbers, cowboys and Indians, "What Will I Be When I Grow Up."

Even activities not usually considered amenable to narrative construction—science, for example—are in fact stories. What is Newtonian physics if it's not the story of what happens between physical bodies close enough and large enough to interact (an idea that occurred to Newton, so the story goes, when an apple fell on his head)? And Einstein's Theory of Relativity can be understood as an alternative reading of the story of nature when we throw a new element into that plot —namely, when we begin to ask what difference does it make to Newton's universe if those forces take time to cause their effects? The story of the universe that emerges from that imaginative reconstruction, that Einsteinian narrative pattern, is in some respects the story of twentieth-century civilization.

Where human beings are, stories are. And where stories are, something fundamentally human is.

II

If it is true that even our most abstruse intellectual endeavors such as theoretical physics can be construed as narrative, then it seems clear that that peculiarly human endeavor we call "art" is even more so. For utilitarians, art is a genuine puzzle to explain unless it can be shown to serve some practical purpose. A utilitarian may collect art but does so primarily for its investment value, its ability to appreciate in monetary worth. The utilitarian is like Soames Forsyte in *The Forsyte Saga*, who knew the price of everything but the value of nothing (including the value of his wife's beauty).

If, however, we are inevitably storytelling animals, then the puzzle of why we place such high value on such a "useless" endeavor as art disappears, because a work of art (among other things) usually tells a story. This is obviously true of the dramatic arts, opera, and most literature. But it is also true in general of the arts that seem less suited to narrative form, such as painting, sculpture, music, and that most utilitarian of all the arts, architecture. Even abstract painting and sculpture and twelve-tone (or no-tone) music tell stories in their own oblique (and sometimes bleak) ways. Perhaps the story they tell is what it's like to be an American or Western European in the last decades of the twentieth century. The iconoclastic pop art of someone like Andy Warhol certainly says a lot about Western consumerism. The seemingly unending stream of sexually ambiguous rock stars says a lot about what William Butler Yeats called "the centre" (which in his opinion was no longer holding, "mere anarchy" having been loosed upon the world). And modern architecture most certainly tells the story of our technological prowess, our ability to build buildings of as many stories as we like.

Of all the modern arts, however, the one that best exemplifies the narrative function of art in general is moving pictures. In deciding on a movie, we always want to know what it's about. That is, we want to know what its story is, what happens in it. Sometimes the way we ask that question is to ask who's in it. If it's Cary Grant and Katharine Hepburn, then we know all we need to know about the story. The same is true if it's Meryl Streep and Robert Redford. Sometimes the way we ask that question is to ask who directed it. And if the answer is Alfred Hitchcock or Steven Spielberg, again we know about as much as we need to know about the story.

Movies have another quality as well. They are probably the most popular art form ever developed. That is, movies are accessible to and appreciated by more people than any other form of art. Rich and poor, literate and unread, movers and shakers, and moved and shaken alike all go to the movies. (It's true that more people watch television, but very little on television can be considered art.) If any modern art can reveal something to us about ourselves or about human nature, it ought to be the movies. I want, therefore, to examine some films, look at their stories, and see if they say anything to us about our own stories. None of the movies I've chosen will ever be considered great art. But for that very reason, they may be even more illuminating in some ways than the great movies of the great masters.

III

One of the most creative and imaginative films ever made was *2001: A Space Odyssey*. It spawned a sequel called *2010: The Year We Make Contact*, which inevitably suffers by comparison with the original film. And truth to tell, it's not nearly as good. However, to be fair to *2010*, we need to avoid comparisons to the earlier one and simply take it on its own terms as a space adventure with few pretensions to theological or philosophical significance (which *2001* had plenty of).

As the title indicates, the action of this film takes place nine years after that of the earlier one. No one seems to know what happened to the mission sent in *2001*, so a new mission to Jupiter is planned to answer that question and, if possible, to retrieve the black monolith that caused everything to happen in the earlier film. This mission is joint U.S.-Soviet venture—the Americans have finally let the Russians in on their big secret. The astronauts get along fine. Unfortunately, their countries don't, and in the middle of the mission, soon after their arrival in orbit around Jupiter, the two crews are ordered by their governments to separate. (It seems as though the United States and the Soviet Union are about to go to war in Central America.)

The American crew transfers to the empty *Discovery I* spaceship of the original mission, which has been orbiting Jupiter these past nine years but is still operational. Now a new crisis arises. The missing astronaut of *2001*, Bowman, appears in ghostly form on the *Discovery I*'s communication monitors to deliver a good news/bad news message. The good news is that "something wonderful" is about to happen. The bad news is that both crews must leave Jupiter or the "something wonderful" will kill them all. Bowman tells them that they have two days to get away. Why is that bad news? Well, it seems as though neither the Soviet nor the American ship has enough fuel to both break out of Jupiter orbit and get back safely to earth. If the ships were to be joined, however, they could together break the orbit and return the two crews safely. The astronauts decide that discretion is the better part of patriotism, rejoin one another in violation of their governments' orders, and manage to break free of Jupiter just before it explodes into a beautiful new star. The Russians and Americans watch in silent wonder as a new part of our solar system is born—a new sun with four planets (the four largest moons of Jupiter; Ganymede, Io, Europa, and Callisto). And as they watch, a message appears on the monitor from an unknown, unidentified source:

All these worlds are yours, except Europa.
Attempt no landing there.
Use them together.
Use them in peace.

The last loose end of the plot is tied up when they receive a communication from earth that their governments have decided that their Central American real estate wasn't worth blowing the world up over and have also realized the need for greater cooperation and understanding.

The story of *2010* is the story of a new creation. It is really a retelling of the Garden of Eden story of the first book of the Bible with the "new heaven, new earth" story of the last book of the Bible. There is a new, pristine creation—the four new planets, the new Eden—created for the human race's enjoyment and use ("All these worlds are yours. . . . Use them together"). But there is a restriction, just as there was in the original paradise—there are to be no attempts to land on Europa and use it. The astronauts will return to earth with this message, which the nations of the earth will accept this time, the movie implies, since the two superpowers, on the very brink of annihilation, have begun to act sanely at last. This new creation may just succeed where the old creation failed. This time, the movie implies, the human race will not succumb to the temptation to eat forbidden fruit. Maybe this new Garden of Eden will not be corrupted by human selfishness and pride, like the old creation was. And maybe the old creation will find redemption in the new—just like the Bible says it will.

IV

Here, then, is a biblical idea that has found its way into a popular movie. On reflection, it's not so implausible to believe that the idea of a new creation should be the basis for a science fiction movie. Also amenable to such treatment is the idea of virgin birth, which is at the center of another science fiction movie, *Starman*. In this film a Starman comes to earth in response to the invitation we issued in 1977 on *Voyager II* (a spaceship which has, by now, escaped our solar system and is somewhere in deep space). The Starman's destination is the Meteor Crater in Arizona, an earlier landing site his race had used. He is deflected from this destination, however, by the U.S. Air Force, which tries to shoot him down. Instead of Meteor Crater, the Starman crash lands in northern Wisconsin and takes the form of a man who had recently died in an accident. The Air Force attack tells him all he needs to know about the inhabitants of earth—we are not yet ready to join the community of intelligent life in the universe. Therefore, he transmits a message to his back-up to rendezvous with him at the Meteor Crater.

The main action of the film has to do with the problem of how he will get from Wisconsin to Arizona. Since he has taken human form, he is now subject to many human limitations. He can't just snap his fingers and be where he wants to be. He persuades the widow of the man whose form he's taken, Jenny Hayden, to drive him to his destination. Unless he arrives within three days, he will be stranded on earth and will die. Jenny is at first terrified of the Starman, who is incarnated in her husband's form, but soon she comes not only to trust him but to love him. In the meantime, the United States government has the FBI, the CIA, the Army, and the Air Force hot on the Starman's trail. Their purpose is to capture him and "study" him—a euphemism for killing him and doing an autopsy. One of the scientists, Mark Sherman, vehemently objects to this program, arguing that we invited him here and don't know that he's hostile or dangerous. His entreaties are to no avail. Jenny quickly realizes that the Starman will not do any harm to us but that we are about to do great harm to him. So, their journey becomes a race to the Meteor Crater in an attempt to thwart the federal authorities. At one point in their flight, Jenny reveals that she is barren. She is physically incapable of having children. The Starman heals her barrenness, impregnating her with a male child. "He will be your child and your husband's," the Starman says, "but he will also be mine. He will know everything I know. When he becomes a man, he will be a teacher." Jenny and the Starman just make it to the Crater (helped by Mark Sherman, even though he knows that his act will cost him his job). As the spaceship slowly ascends with the rescued Starman, a heavenly benediction gently falls on Jenny, confirming her worthiness to be the mother of the Starman's child.

Again, we see a basic similarity to the biblical pattern in this movie. This is the annunciation to Mary; it's the story of the Incarnation and virgin birth in contemporary form. Jenny Hayden, like Mary, receives a supernatural visitor. Jenny Hayden, like Mary, cannot have a child. Jenny Hayden, like Mary, does become pregnant (in spite of the impossibility), and like Mary, she will give birth to a son who will be possessed of supernatural wisdom and power. The Starman, like Jesus, is a healer and a giver of life. His supernatural powers can save others, but he cannot save himself. His human offspring will also be a healer who will save others. The Starman's son will be human, but he will be more than human. Ordinary human beings are in the main fearful and hostile toward others and are, therefore, best at taking life, not giving it. The Starman's son, in contrast, will not use coercion, but will be a teacher who uses gentle persuasion and the power of ideas. Will the human race of the future listen to such a message? Well, already at least some human beings have good impulses that enhance rather than threaten life. Jenny Hayden's love overcomes her fear, so she helps the Starman escape. Mark Sherman's sense of right and wrong is stronger than his self-interest, and he lets the Starman go, even though it will cost him his job and his career. The Incarnation/virgin birth pattern is a way of saying that there is a supernatural aiding and abetting of our good impulses to help them become dominant in our lives.

In *Indiana Jones and the Temple of Doom*—on the whole an unpromising and unlikely film because its main characters are nasty and mean-spirited people—we nevertheless have a profoundly moving moment when all the children who have been enslaved in the Temple of Doom rush around Indiana Jones, holding their manacled arms up, clamoring for him to free them.

As Jones unlocks their chains, we feel for just a moment at least that the natural human condition is freedom, not slavery. And this extraordinary scene reminds us that the God of the Bible is a liberating God, who unchains manacled captives and tears down walls of separation.

And in *Places in the Heart* we see three very different people —a widow, confused by her husband's tragic death, innocent of the ways of the world, but a fast learner; a black man who has made his way in the world by deception and thievery (since the world offers him no better options); and a blind man, bitter because of his blindness—who come together in their mutual need and find redemption in the community they create by working toward a common, worthwhile goal.

V

We could go on with virtually any movie and probably find something similar to say even in the most unpromising. If we did so, I think we would discover that among all these different stories there is really only one basic story—the story of the conflict between good and evil. In each of the films I've mentioned, human beings are placed in situations that threaten their well-being. In each case they are faced with a decision to act either for their own narrow self-interest or for what they know to be the best. In each case they choose the good over the bad, life over death and destruction. The astronauts cooperate with one another in spite of political differences; Jenny Hayden and Mark Sherman decide to trust the Starman instead of fear him; Indiana Jones (for all his macho egocentrism) frees the children, etc.

We leave the theater after such movies feeling pretty good, at least for awhile, reassured that good does triumph over evil. Unfortunately the real world that impinges immediately on us as we try to leave the theater parking lot unscathed seems less malleable to such a message, and the glow of good feeling pretty well fades after watching the late night news or reading the next morning's headlines. Whether we say so to ourselves or not, most of us probably feel, "Well, it was just a story," by which we mean, of course, that it's not real. That is, most of us don't really believe in the power of good in its conflict with evil. Most of us are probably really pessimists or skeptics or cynics deep down inside, though deep down inside we don't really want to be that. We really want to believe in good.

"It was just a story." Of course, movies are just stories. But before we become dismissive, we ought to consider what we're saying. Movies may be just stories, but then so are a lot of other things that we would never be so cavalier about. What about your life and my life? Isn't it true that every human being writes at least one story, the story of his or her life? Buechner says that we all are writing our own stories. Furthermore, Buechner says that the story of any one of us is in some sense the story of us all. My story, with all its particularity and peculiarity, is in some sense also your story. Buechner writes stories, most of them fiction with made-up characters like Tristram Bone and Ansel Gibbs and Leo Bebb, but some of them with real characters like St. Godric and Frederick Buechner. Are some of these stories real because they happen to be about historical people who actually lived, while others are not real because they happen to be about people Buechner thought up in his imagination? We certainly want to keep some such distinction in mind for our everyday discourse with each other. But all of us are Platonists enough to believe that some narrative patterns, at least, whether they are about real or imagined characters, are themselves real.

So, just because something is a story doesn't mean that it's *just* a story. If a movie or play or work of fiction about imagined characters helps us understand our lives, your story and mine, isn't it just as real in its own way as, say, Buechner's autobiography, which does the same thing? Buechner candidly told his own story in *The Sacred Journey*, and *Now and Then*, and *Telling Secrets* because he believed that retelling his story would illuminate that of his readers, would help them see the pattern of their lives. The lesson, consequently, is that we ought to listen carefully to the stories around us, even the fictional ones, even the ones in movies, because they may very well be our own.

So, what about your story; what about the story you're writing, which you call your life? How does your story fit in with the big story that all other stories are merely variations of? How does your story fit in with the story of the conflict between good and evil? To put our lives in these terms is pretty daunting and maybe even discouraging, because we tend to think that the fight against evil must be heroic and cosmic in scale. That's why the words of Jesus in Matthew 10:42 are so comforting. Whoever gives a cup of cold water for Jesus' sake to someone who is thirsty is helping bring the reign of God in. Giving a cup of cold water does that? That's what Jesus said. What I think he meant is that the smallest acts of kindness and self-giving, where our focus is on the needs of others rather than ourselves, are as much a contribution as the large acts of goodness that get recorded in the history books.

I'm no Francis of Assisi or George Fox or Gandhi or Martin Luther King, Jr. But God doesn't expect me to do what these great moral leaders did. All God expects of me is that I give a cup of cold water to the thirsty. What about you? What's your story? You don't have to be a hero or heroine to make your story count.

Notes

1. Kathryn Morton, "The Story-Telling Animal," the *New York Times Book Review*, vol. LXXXIX, No. 52, December 23, 1984, 1.
   2. Ibid.

Madison Avenue Salvation

Matthew 6:25-33

I

Television is ubiquitous in America. There's scarcely any public place we can go these days without encountering television monitors of some sort. Not even the church has escaped this phenomenon, for if you go to Robert Schuller's Crystal Cathedral in Anaheim, California, you'll discover that the dominant focus of attention in the sanctuary is a giant instant-replay screen off to the right of the congregation. I won't venture to prophesy whether or not this is the wave of the future in Christian worship, but our imaginations do not have to be overly creative to envision—as Schuller would certainly want us to—the Possibilities.

This ubiquity of television has a corollary—namely, the omnipresence of television commercials. Except for the public channels, everything we see on television is sponsored by some company engaged in a commercial endeavor. These companies buy time in order to get us, the viewers, to buy their product or use their service. The commercials they produce, like the shows they sponsor, are some very good, some very bad, and some somewhere in between.

The bad commercials are truly bad, some of the tackiest things we will ever see on TV. Frankly, I don't care how many people squeeze the Charmin. And waxy yellow build-up on the kitchen linoleum is not comparable to, say, the problem of the federal deficit or the likelihood of nuclear war. Particularly offensive is the way these tacky commercials portray women, who apparently have nothing greater to worry about than "ring around the collar" or "static cling."

I must admit, however, that some commercials are very good—

in fact, some commercials are better and more interesting than the programs they sponsor. They exhibit high production values, tell a coherent story in thirty seconds, create identifiable characters, and are often genuinely funny.

II

All commercials convey the basic message that when we have a problem or a need, this product or that service will solve the problem or meet the need. There are, for example, that husband and wife in the Chevrolet commercial who have a serious disagreement about which car to buy.

"I like small cars," he says.

"We need a big car," she counters, gesturing toward their three growing children in the background.

Clearly, if they can't agree on the right car, this couple will soon need some serious marriage counseling. Chevrolet, however, helps avert this crisis by transporting this couple along with their three growing children into a midsized Chevrolet that (presumably) combines all the advantages the husband wanted in a small car with all the room the wife insisted they needed in a big car. (The three kids in the back are actually smiling at each other, they have so much room.)

Then, there is that besieged shipping clerk who has three superiors command him to get three packages to three different locations by 10:30 A.M. the following day using three different shippers. The shipping clerk is obviously smarter than his three bosses, because he ignores their orders, calls Federal Express, and loafs the rest of the day, secure in his knowledge that Federal Express will get all three jobs done and his bosses will be none the wiser.

In a hurry for a meal? Then "Try Burger King now!" And if you don't care for Burger King Whoppers, there's always McDonald's, Wendy's, Arby's, Hardees, Kentucky Fried Chicken, Maryland Fried Chicken, Bojangles' and Popeye's *Famous* Fried Chicken, Long John Silver's, Moby Dick, Pizza Hut, Domino's, Taco Tico, Taco Bell, Taco Mayo, and many, many more. Any of these will get you a meal fast, and some of them will even deliver it directly to your door.

No one makes us buy any of these things, and a commercial does let us know they're available (just in case we have a Big

Mac attack). Commercials are simply a ubiquitous part of twentieth-century American culture.

III

Some commercials, however, send us not only the basic
message that a certain product or service is available if we need
it. They also—some of them—send a more subtle message that
this product or service can make us happy, can satisfy our
deepest longings or desires. All we really need for ultimate
fulfillment is this car or that cologne. If we drink this wine or
shave with this razor or protect ourselves with this deodorant,
all our hearts' desires will be ours.

This promise of happiness comes in various guises. Commercials are never as blatant in their claims as I have just put it. Some
commercials use the term *success* or one of its synonyms, such
as *winning*. In one Chevrolet commercial, for example, there's a
young man standing on some bleachers in a crowd, enthusiasti-
cally cheering his team on at some unidentified athletic contest.
The camera moves in on him, and the omniscient voice-over
says, "You look like you're into winning." This young man
immediately forgets the athletic contest and nods vigorous as-
sent. Then—just like the couple with the three children—he is
instantly translated to the driver's seat of a small Chevrolet,
where he runs his hand lovingly across the seat with an expression of deep satisfaction on his face. The young man never utters
a word; the godlike, invisible narrator is the only voice we hear,
but the young man's smiling satisfaction says as well as words
could, "Yes, this is what I need to be a winner."

There's another Chevrolet commercial about the executive (in
his late thirties or early forties) promoted to vice president of his
company by a silver-haired, benevolent father figure (in his late
fifties or early sixties). Along with the VP sign for his desk comes
a set of keys to a full-size luxury Chevrolet, which seems to drive
to the country club and social success almost by itself.

Success may be construed in terms of power—as in commercials for sports cars and motorcycles and pickup trucks. Or, it
may be couched in terms of social acceptance and popularity—
especially with members of the opposite sex. Remember that
balding, pudgy, middle-aged Aldo Cella has beautiful young
women hanging *on* his arms because *in* his arms he carries

bottles of Cella wine. Or success may be expressed in terms of in-group/out-group sociology. All of us want to be a part of the Pepsi Generation, don't we? Obviously Pepsi Generation people are the right kind of people, the kind of people you and I want to be. And who would not want to own a Cadillac? In commercials we see Cadillacs only at the country club, the country estate, the theater, or in front of a yacht.

Quite clearly the message of these commercials is: Buy this car, drink this wine, use this soap or detergent, wear these clothes—and you will be somebody, and everyone else will recognize that you are somebody. This is the Gospel according to Madison Avenue; this is Madison Avenue Salvation.

IV

The result of the extraordinary point of view in such commercials is the depersonalizing of human nature. The implicit assumption of such commercials is that human nature should be defined in terms of the products it consumes. Who am I? According to the Madison Avenue Gospel, I am the Consumer. I am what I consume. And this assumption has a further implication, which I have already touched on—namely, the more significant and expensive the product consumed, the more important I must be. Who am I? Not just the consumer. Rather, I am the Consumer of Significant Things. I am the Cadillac owner, who drinks Paul Masson Special Reserve wines, who wears Hickey-Freeman suits and Gucci shoes and Countess Mara ties, who tells time by my Rolex watch, whose woman (it doesn't necessarily have to be my wife) is sexually alluring because she (like Catherine Deneuve) uses Chanel No. 5. If I have all these things, then I must be somebody—right? Other people must respect me and listen to my opinions, which must be worthwhile—correct? My interests should take precedence over those of people who don't have these things—shouldn't they?

Some commercials state explicitly this usually implicit assumption (that I am nothing but what I consume) by having the human being in the commercial actually turn into the product advertised. One motorcycle commercial has a silhouetted human figure move to a crouching position with arms extended straight out in front, and then, magically, like a Gobot, the human figure turns into the motorcycle. And some sports car commercials speak of the melding of "man and machine."

Perhaps no commercials express this dehumanization, this trivializing of human nature, better than the ones for fast food. Have you ever seen a hamburger or pizza or fried chicken commercial where the customer does not have a look of transcendent, ecstatic joy on his or her face while eating? Eating a Big Mac is, apparently, a matchless, sublime experience. Consuming a pizza seems to be the ultimate religious ecstasy. Kentucky Fried Chicken with its secret recipe of eleven herbs and spices will, it appears, produce the gustatory equivalent of orgasm. The people presented in these commercials experience total joy, complete fulfillment, ultimate satisfaction.

This dehumanization is bad enough. From a Christian perspective such a message is even worse because it is essentially idolatrous. This point may not be so obvious since we aren't dealing with little statues or gold-plated representations of bulls—our Cecil B. DeMille conception of an idol. In biblical terms, an idol is anything that becomes more important to us than God and, thus, anything that keeps us from God. When a commercial implies that some product or service will give complete satisfaction for our deepest needs, it makes that product or service into an idol. It claims an ultimacy for a finite thing that no finite thing can ever have. It tells us, implicitly, that all that really counts is things and that getting the best things we can is the most important way to live our lives. Idolatry of this sort is wrong because it keeps us from God. When material things become idols, they are bad, not because they're material things, but because they have deflected us from our true good, that which gives us life, God.

V

The Christian response to the idolatrous consumerism of our culture is found in these words of Jesus that culminated his teaching on material things: "Set your mind on God's kingdom and his justice before everything else, and all the rest will come to you as well" (Matthew 6:33, REB). If we have our priorities right, Jesus says, then we will not be bothered by the idolatrous allure of material things.

So, how do we seek the reign of God in the midst of a culture given over to excessive consumerism? This question deserves a whole book, but all we can give it is a few words. The first word is this. True human fulfillment comes only from God. Things we consume will never satisfy our deepest longings and needs. Jesus said we should put God's reign first and, if we do, then everything else we need would be ours. Saint Augustine said, "Thou has made us for Thyself, and our hearts are restless till they find their rest in Thee." And one of the catechisms begins with this question and answer: "What is the chief end of humans? To glorify God and enjoy God forever." To be fully what we were created to be requires that we reject our culture's assumption that consuming things will bring us happiness. It requires us to witness to our culture, in the way we use material things, that our culture's values are wrong. In our deepest heart of hearts we need God, we have been born to love God, and our ultimate purpose is to find our deepest satisfaction in God. As the catechism says, we are to enjoy God, not things, forever.

The second word, paradoxically, is this. We ought to accept our culture for what it is, recognizing that without God there is really nowhere else to turn but to things. What I mean is that our culture, with its excessive consumerism, is simply following to its logical end the implication of its starting premise. If we begin with the premise that life is nothing more than food and clothing and consumable goods, then obviously the best life will be the one that consumes the most and has the best. If we are what we consume, then we are at our best when we consume the best. What else can we expect from a world that doesn't know God? Let us go as far with the world as we can without giving up or compromising our first love. Let us praise and encourage the creative drive within us that leads us to turn the created order into things for our human welfare and enjoyment. But let us also say to the world that life is more than meat, and the body more than raiment.

And the third word, like the second, is also a paradox. We ought to develop a willing detachment from things, an attitude that hangs loose with regard to our possessions and our material existence in the world. This willing detachment is paradoxical because, on the one hand, we are called to love the world with the same passionate concern God demonstrated in sending Jesus to save the world. But on the other, we are called to be prepared

There is another, different attitude of despair we might adopt. I call it "heroic cosmic despair." It embodies the despair we experience when we realize that anything we value has no permanence, but it does not degenerate into the "eat, drink, and be merry" variety. No, the one who despairs heroically still clings to the values we all share—truth, beauty, goodness, justice—but does so as an act of heroic (though ultimately futile) defiance against an indifferent or, possibly, malevolent universe. The hero of cosmic despair says, in effect: "I know that what I value will not last. It will one day be destroyed. I know that truth, beauty, justice, goodness are doomed in the last analysis to be frustrated and thwarted. But I thumb my nose at the universe and its indifference. I will continue to live my life in accordance with these values, even though I know I'm doomed to defeat." No one put this attitude better than Bertrand Russell in an early essay entitled "A Free Man's Worship":

> That man is the product of causes which had no prevision of the end they were achieving; that his origin, his growth, his hopes and fears, his loves and his beliefs, are but the outcome of accidental collocations of atoms; that no fire, no heroism, no intensity of thought and feeling, can preserve an individual life beyond the grave; that all the labors of the ages, all the devotion, all the inspiration, all the noonday brightness of human genius, are destined to extinction in the vast death of the solar system, and that the whole temple of man's achievement must inevitably be buried beneath the debris of a universe in ruins—all these things, if not quite beyond dispute, are yet so nearly certain that no philosophy which rejects them can hope to stand. Only within the scaffolding of these truths, only on the firm foundation of unyielding despair, can the soul's habitation henceforth be safely built.[2]

No one had a keener sense about social and political justice than Russell. And no one worked harder to make the world a better place than he did. Yet he did so believing that all of his efforts would eventually come to nought. "Unyielding despair," he says, must be our attitude, the only "firm foundation" on which to build our lives.

Living in an age of transition threatens us because it threatens that which we value most. We know that one day our earth and everything in it will be destroyed. We may respond like the reactionary and try to hold change back or pretend that it is not there. Or, we may respond with cosmic despair—either in its nihilistic or heroic forms. If these were our only choices, I hope I would opt for heroic cosmic despair like Russell's.

But we have not yet said all there is to say about the future, change, and threats to what we value.

IV

John 20 portrays Mary Magdalene as one threatened by cosmic despair. Her world has crumbled. What she valued most—her relationship to Jesus—has been destroyed by death. She is sorrowful and grief-stricken. She weeps. The risen Christ approaches her, and she doesn't even recognize him. Her cry is the cry of despair: "The one who meant the most to me, the one whom I loved the most, is gone. He's dead. I'll never see him again. And I don't even know where his body is so that I can honor his memory." She is saying that what she most valued has been taken from her and that she no longer has anything to live for.

Jesus speaks her name, and with that one word she realizes that he is not dead but alive and standing before her. What she cherished most in this world has not been destroyed after all. In joy she reaches out for Jesus to take hold of him and never let him go. But Jesus stops her. "Do not cling to me," he says, "for I have not yet ascended to God." And then Jesus gives Mary a commission: "Go and tell my brothers that I am ascending to God." Mary is ordained to be the first witness to the Resurrection. She is ordained to be the first evangelist, the first bearer of Good News. So Mary goes to the disciples and says, "I have seen the Lord!" Her message is that what they all had valued most in this world had not been destroyed or taken from them after all.

V

This is Good News. But there is more to Jesus' message than this. There is also the command to accept the fact of change. "Do not cling to me," Jesus says to Mary, when she reaches out to grab hold of Jesus and never let him go. "What I have meant to you has not been lost," Jesus is saying, "but what I have meant to you is being changed. I am ascending to God. So, you must not try to cling to me, to hold on to what our relationship was. If you truly want to preserve my value to you, then you must let the old relationship go and accept the new reality of my resurrection. Nothing essential between us has changed. But there are changes, and you must accept them, or you will run the risk of losing everything."

The resurrection of Jesus shows that what we value most, if it is what we ought most to value, persists through change. What we value changes, but nothing essential is lost. I do not know how this can be. I do not know how the value of great works of art and literature and music will be preserved. I do not know how people we have loved—parents, children, friends—continue to be real values after the death of their bodies. I have confidence, however, that value—our highest and best values— are preserved, though transformed. And I have this confidence because this is what happened to Jesus. Jesus died. But death did not destroy him. He lives, and he is still with us as our highest value.

Therefore, we need not despair that our work for goodness and beauty and justice is in vain, whether or not we are successful. In some way that we cannot fathom, God will make sure that what we do will be of lasting value. We can have confidence that even the smallest act of rightness makes some difference and will not be lost. But if we cling desperately to the old embodiments of value, we will miss the new. Faith in Christ means the willingness to let go of the past in order to have the future. It means the willingness to undergo the transformation from something old to something new, something wonderful. We must lose in order to find.

"All's lost," Godric says at the end of his life, as he realizes that he is about to die and finally meet God face to face. But then he says, "All's found."[3] Godric had to give up his life in order to find it. Another saint put it this way: "If anyone is in Christ, there is a new creation; everything old has passed away; see, everything has become new!" (2 Corinthians 5:17).

Notes

1. Raziel Abelson and Marie-Louise Friquegnon, *Ethics for Modern Life*, 2nd ed. (New York: St. Martin's Press, 1982), 4-5.

2. Bertrand Russell, *Why I Am Not a Christian and Other Essays*

on Religion and Related Subjects (New York: Simon and Schuster, 1957), 107.

3. Frederick Buechner, *Godric* (New York: Atheneum, 1980), 171.

Canine Metaphysics

John 3:16-17

I

It used to be that whenever people began talking about their pets (how sweet, how cute, but especially how intelligent they are), I began looking for a discreet way to become absent. I simply didn't believe that any "dumb animal" could be quite as glorious as its owner made out. And furthermore, I suspected that the pet owner was engaging in an anthropomorphism that would make even a biblical writer blush.

Well, mea culpa. I recant my heresy. I was wrong.

The agent of this conversion experience is a Yorkshire terrier we acquired as a puppy a few years ago, which we named Terrie. Terrie has now entered into a state of permanent canine adolescence, which dog psychologists say is normal (so we don't feel too bad about the way she turned out). When she was a puppy, we kept her in the kitchen with gates across the entrances to minimize the destruction of our personal property when we were gone.

Like all pet owners, I consider my pet to be almost human and, of course, very intelligent. She's smart enough, for example, to know when to be dumb about certain things we want her to learn that she has decided she doesn't want to learn. When we are instructing her on one of these vital matters, she has a way of cocking her head to one side with a puzzled look on her face, saying through her body language, "You want me to do *what*?"

Her recalcitrance, however, is not the way I usually think of her. More characteristic is the way she used to greet us when we approached the kitchen and her reaction when we left. When she heard us approaching, she would come to the gate, stretching up as far as she could, placing her forepaws over the top of the gate, wagging her tail (such as it is) furiously, sniffing the air continuously, and darting her dark brown eyes up and down and all around. She was quite clearly searching for some clue that would indicate our intent—were we coming to play with her or do something else? Naturally she hoped we were coming to play. And the disappointment in her eyes was palpable if we didn't.

But her reaction when we left was even more intense. If Her Majesty felt we had not paid her the proper obeisance, she would rear up on her hind legs, clasp us somewhere about the knee with her forelegs, and embrace us with all the energy and desperate hope of a rejected lover. If she could have spoken English, she could not more clearly have said to us, "Don't go, stay and play with me, give me your attention."

The remarkable thing about our pet is that she never asked for the absolute necessities of life, food and water, when she was a puppy. But she has quite clearly and consistently asked for our time. She seems to know, in her own canine way, that love and attention and physical intimacy are as necessary as food and water.

II

And that observation of my dog has set me to thinking: perhaps love is the most important thing in the world. Such an idea is dismissed as mawkish sentimentality by the cynics and hard-headed realists who run the world. But no one can deny its appeal.

It appealed, for example, to the pre-Socratic philosopher Empedocles, who believed that the ultimate source of everything is love and strife. These two forces explain the universe and everything in it. Love, Empedocles asserted, causes things to come together and form unities. Strife, in contrast, causes things to fall apart and dissolve into their individual components. Sometimes love predominates, and then the world is a good and beautiful place. Sometimes, however, strife predominates, and then the world is evil and ugly and full of tension, conflict, and war. Clearly we ought to prefer the world caused by love to that caused by strife.

We might be tempted to dismiss Empedocles because he was an ancient philosopher still very much influenced by ancient mythology. But we cannot use the same argument to dismiss C.S. Peirce, one of the greatest of American philosophers, probably the most influential American thinker of the nineteenth century. Peirce was educated at Harvard in mathematics, physics, and chemistry. Rather than practice science, however, he preferred to work out the intellectual implications of science. Peirce was, in other words, a philosopher of science. He argued that only the scientific method was adequate to answer our questions. And he was an early champion of evolutionary theory, which was just beginning to come into its own in his day.

He does not sound like a promising candidate for a champion of the primacy of love. Yet, in spite of his scientific training and predilections, when he came to the question of how evolution worked, he decided that the best term to describe this process was *agapastic*—an ugly word for a lovely idea. *Agapastic* is an adjective form of the noun *agape*, which, as we all know, is the New Testament concept of Christian love, the self-giving love that puts others first and that is best exemplified in God's love for us in Christ. Peirce concluded that evolution must be agapastic because only this kind of love could account for the widest variety of being while at the same time accounting for the continuity and interdependence that we actually observe in the process. In other words, the basic process by which the universe evolves is self-giving love.

This idea has blossomed in the twentieth century in what we call Process Philosophy and Process Theology. Some of the Process thinkers conceive of God as the supremely lovely Reality, out ahead of the created order (which is unfinished as yet and still in the process of being created), luring the universe on to achieve more and more of its good potential. God is the great lover who seduces the cosmos to greater perfection, until one day it will be complete in God.

But we don't have to remain in the rarefied atmosphere of philosophy and theology to see this idea of everything in the universe capable of and needing love. We can find it in popular culture as well. We've all seen the bumper sticker that asks, "Have you hugged your kid today?" And, of course, popular music is full of this idea: "What the world needs now/Is love, sweet love. It's the only thing/That there's just too little of." Or:

"Let there be peace on earth. And let it begin with me." Psychologists and social workers say that unmarried teen-age girls who get pregnant do not really want sex, but rather want to be held, embraced, loved.

And in *The Color Purple*, Shug Avery tells Celie that everything wants "to be loved. . . . You ever notice that trees do everything to git attention we do, except walk?"[1]

Everything wants to be loved. And that's why trees put on their new duds in the spring, and that's why in the fall they are brilliant with color. If they could, they would even walk and dance and prance around for us, saying to us, "Look at me. I am part of the goodness of creation, just like you."

III

When I encounter such phenomena as these, all apparently saying the same thing, I begin looking for some underlying point of view which they all share. In other words, I begin looking for their "metaphysic." Furthermore, I want to give this implicit point of view a name that will help me identify it when I encounter it again. So, I propose to call this point of view implicit in all these phenomena I've catalogued—my dog's behavior, those philosophies and theologies, our culture of bumper stickers and popular music and literature—the "organic view of reality."

One who adopts this organic view of reality sees an underlying connectedness among all things and a commonality of interest and concerns, so that nothing is really foreign to anything else, regardless of how different things seem to be. One who adopts this point of view is uneasy dividing the world up into separate and distinct categories that imply that things have little or no relatedness—the animate and the inanimate, for example. Instead, from this point of view there is the tendency to see the (presumably) lower orders in terms of the (presumably) higher orders with a seamless web of continuity running from one to the other. Consider the terms I used to describe my dog—*adolescence, intelligence, puzzlement, recalcitrance, searching for some clue, disappointment, desperate hope, rejected lover*. I understand and describe my dog's behavior in terms of human behavior. And this is a perfectly natural and normal way to talk. In fact, without using these anthropomorphic terms, I could not understand my dog at all. So, what seems to be true for human beings also seems to be true for "dumb animals," if to a lesser extent.

The organic view of reality sees everything in the universe as alive and growing in some sense, developing into something more than it now is and contributing (for good or ill) to the whole. If Christians hold this view, they will add something further and say along with Gerard Manley Hopkins, "The world is charged with the grandeur of God." In other words, everything that is reflects somehow, to one degree or another, the divine reality. From "lowest" to "highest" in the order of creation we can see a reflection of God, if we look for it. And what of the wild variety and diversity of creation, the oppositions of hot and cold, wet and dry, living and nonliving, conscious and nonconscious? Hopkins has a Christian word about that, too, in "Pied Beauty":

> All things counter, original, spare, strange;
>> Whatever is fickle, freckled (who knows how?)
>> With swift, slow; sweet, sour; adazzle, dim;
> He fathers-forth whose beauty is past change:
>>> Praise him.[2]

This organic view of reality has some ethical consequences as well. If all things are potentially alive and if all contribute to the fulfillment of the whole, then we must learn to respect all things for what they are. Nothing in the world will be seen as something merely for our use. Instead, we will recognize its integrity and value and right to be. In addition to this attitude of respect, we will also begin developing a high level of consciousness regarding the way our actions affect other things. We will consider the consequences to the larger community (human and nonhuman), and this consideration will play a significant part in the decisions we make. This point of view means, of course, that on many occasions we will even forego satisfying our desires because to do so would be to violate the integrity of some other part of the universe. This view stresses harmony, unity, respect, the mutual good of all. There is even a reverence for all things, for everything is "charged with the grandeur of God. . . . Praise God."

IV

This organic view of reality is not the only one, of course, and today it's not even the dominant one. In sharp contrast to it is what I call the "atomic view of reality." This view asserts that the universe consists of discrete, distinct, particular things—atoms—that have no essential interconnectedness except when they happen to run into each other. The model for this view is the "billiard ball" model of the atom—the comparison of atoms to billiard balls on a billiard table. Each ball represents an atom, and the table represents empty space. All atoms are pictured as discrete, isolated particles in motion. Eventually some of them (like billiard balls) collide with others, and the stronger of the two forces determines the outcome. The atoms may just bounce off each other, or they may combine in some temporary, unstable form to make a larger discrete particular. (Here the billiard ball analogy doesn't work.) Maybe one destroys the other. In any case, the basic model is one of conflict—one external force operating on another external force, each attempting to be the dominant force.

Notice how this model gets transferred from natural science to human affairs and determines our way of looking at ourselves and others. Think, for a moment, of the dominant image that controls our understanding of international relations, the image of "the balance of power." Nation X has influence in area A, so nation Y must seek to counter-balance that influence by becoming powerful in area B. This atomic view of reality was the underlying intellectual assumption of the Cold War.

It also undergirds our behavior in other important areas of life. Business leaders justify unscrupulous business practices by saying, "It's a dog-eat-dog world." (Have you ever seen one dog eat another dog?) One of the most popular books of a few years back was Robert Ringer's *Looking Out for Number One.* And William Safire has written a syndicated column extolling the virtues of greed, asserting that it should be dropped from the catalog of the seven deadly sins. His argument was the utilitarian one that greed had done a lot of good, producing wealth and jobs and general prosperity. J.R. Ewing, I suppose, becomes the model for such behavior; after all, J.R. did provide jobs for some of the denizens of Dallas.

Clearly this atomic view of reality has its ethical implications, just like the organic view. If we adopt this second view, our concern will be mainly for ourselves and our own interests. We will not be particularly concerned about the way our action affects others. If what we do has good consequences for others, fine. But if it has bad consequences, then that's fine too, as long as we achieve our own goals. (Or, maybe it's not fine; maybe it's too bad, and maybe we feel sorry that someone else is hurt by our decisions. But it's really not our concern—we got what we wanted.) This ethic is best expressed in Milton Friedman's essay "The Social Responsibility of Business Is to Increase Its Profits."[3] Friedman, the contemporary guru of laissez-faire capitalism, argues that the only ethical duty of a business executive is to return as great a profit as possible on the investment. An executive, according to Friedman, has no ethical responsibility to make decisions that attain worthwhile social goals (such as moderating inflation or reducing pollution).

It seems to me that underlying all these examples—international power politics, the justification of greed, laissez-faire capitalism—is the atomic view of reality. It seems to me that the only way one can maintain such positions is to implicitly believe there is no essential interconnection among all things. It doesn't matter, then, what the consequences of our behavior are for other people or for the physical environment, as long as we get our way. This atomic view of reality is seen in a common attitude toward people on poverty rolls:

"Why don't they work?" we ask with exasperation.

"Well, they can't get jobs because they don't have enough education."

"Well, why don't they go to school and get an education?"

"Because they live in the inner city where the schools aren't any good."

"Why don't they move out of the inner city to a nice neighborhood where they'll have good schools?"

"Fine, except they can't afford to do that."

"Well, if they'd get a job they could."

"Sure. And by the way, would you want them moving next door to you?"

"Don't be absurd! I've got to think of the value of my investment."

V

It's always an oversimplification to say that for a given topic there are two and only two views that are mutually inconsistent and incompatible. In fact, every different view of things has points in common with opposing views. And this is probably true with the organic and atomic views of reality. Nevertheless, they are different, and they are—in the last analysis—opposed to one another. Both can be found in the Bible, in various guises, so the Bible's authority can be cited for either as justification. Yet, it seems to me that the main thrust of the biblical revelation is on the side of the organic view of reality. The Bible clearly reveals a God who created the world and saw that that creation was good in every way. Clearly, God loves the world, even when it has gone wrong. God loves the world so much that God has gone to inordinate lengths to redeem the world from its lostness and make it whole again. The most famous verses in the Bible read, "For God so loved the world that he gave his only Son, so that everyone who believes in him may not perish but may have eternal life. Indeed, God did not send the Son into the world to condemn the world, but in order that the world might be saved through him" (John 3:16-17).

We often read the first of these verses but forget about the second. We stress the "whosoever believeth in him" so much that we forget that the purpose for which God sent the Son was to save the world, the whole world, and that the motive for this great act of salvation was agape, self-giving, self-sacrificing love, whose primary concern is the well-being of the other. The whole world is the creation of God (from "lowest" to "highest"), and the whole world is the object of God's self-giving love and God's saving acts. This says to me that the world God created is an organic whole, a unity, a seamless web of reality in which one part is intimately interconnected with every other part. So you can't just save part of it and let the rest of it go. If sin and corruption have infected all of the universe, then salvation and redemption are also infecting all the universe as well.

We are all part of one another—I believe this is what the Bible teaches. And that means, of course, that my dog's insistence on being loved is in keeping with God's purposes in creating her and the color purple and trees and rocks and clouds and comets and planets and galaxies and you and me. Why, then, do we call animals like my dog "dumb"? She actually knows the secret of the universe—that agape love is the ultimate reality and that we were created to live that love. And that means she's actually smarter than a lot of us.

Notes

1. Alice Walker, *The Color Purple* (New York: Washington Square Press, 1983), 178-179.

2. Walter E. Houghton and G. Robert Stange, *Victorian Poetry and Poetics*, (Boston: Houghton Mifflin Co., 1959), 673.

3. Milton Friedman, "The Social Responsibility of Business Is to Increase Its Profits" in Raziel Abelson and Marie-Louise Friquegnon, *Ethics for Modern Life*, 2nd ed. (New York: St. Martin's Press, 1982), 318-324.

A Happy New Year in the Peaceable Kingdom

Isaiah 2:2-4; 11:1-9
Luke 12:22-32; 17:20-21

I

"Happy New Year."

How many times have you heard these words lately? How many times have you said these words lately? Saying "Happy New Year" is a social ritual we all engage in at this time of year, with hardly a thought about the meaning of the words.

"Happy New Year."

I spend most of my time between Christmas and New Year's on the phone, making appointments with accounts, making motel and airline reservations. The people I do business with have all been wishing me a "Happy New Year." "Yes, and a Happy New Year to you, too," I respond.

Wishing people a Happy New Year is, as I said, a social ritual we all do without much thought. Perhaps not thinking about what these words mean is a defense mechanism on our part, because the truth is that the world does not seem a very happy place right now. Prospects for happiness in this new year of our Lord seem pretty dim. The mood we feel now is a stark contrast to the mood we were feeling just a few years ago.

Do you remember just a few years ago? The words our public pundits were using not so long ago were *euphoria*, the *peace dividend*, the *triumph of freedom*, the *downfall of tyranny*. Those were heady days, not so long ago, when the possibility that the new year might really be a happy one seemed very real. We had witnessed things we thought we would never see. The Berlin Wall, that old symbol of much of our unhappiness, had come down, and the two Germanys were going to reunite.

Apartheid in South Africa was crumbling, and a dignified Nelson Mandela had made his way triumphantly through the Western democracies. Eastern dictatorships were falling like dominoes, and the Soviet Union, that old evil empire, was restructuring itself in an unprecedented new era of openness.

And in Beijing, China, we watched unbelievingly as a lone, frail, defenseless student stood his ground in front of an approaching Chinese tank and brought the tank to a halt. Do you remember how good it felt, not so long ago, because we in the West were saying that we had finally won? The rest of the world wanted to be like us!

II

The contrast between recent new years and those of the late 1980s could hardly be sharper. We no longer talk of *euphoria* or *peace dividends* or *the end of tyranny and dictatorship.* The Germans on both sides of the defunct Berlin Wall have discovered how really difficult and costly reunification will be. Reactionary racist movements in South Africa are on the rise. The Soviet Union has disintegrated into multi-ethnic states that seem determined not to get along with each other. Yugoslavia has tried to commit suicide. And we all know what happened in Beijing, China, just a few days after that lone, frail, defenseless student stopped that tank dead in its tracks. We call what happened Tiananmen Square.

If we want to date the end of this era of good feeling, we could make a good case for August 2, 1990, when Iraq invaded Kuwait, plunging our world into yet one more international crisis. Of course, all along there has been an undercurrent of dis-ease about problems that just don't want to go away—the continuing degradation of our environment, our declining economy, the chasmlike disparity between rich and poor, the federal deficit, the savings and loan scandal, the banking crisis, and on and on.

"Happy New Year."

My wife and I went to a party December 31, 1990. If these global problems were not depressing enough, some of the personal problems of some of our friends were. One couple had a son serving in an elite combat unit in Saudi Arabia, and his prospect for survival was one of the unspoken subjects of our conversation. (He did survive.) Another couple needed to talk about the disillusionment their son, a college junior, was feeling at the greed and selfishness he witnessed among his own generation. A third couple came late because they had to check one of their sons, who was suffering a deep depression, into Our Lady of Peace.

For these friends, there was a real question whether the new year, 1991, would be happy or not. Our mood at the beginning of that particular new year was less like that of Isaiah 2 and more like that of Joel 3:9-10:

> *"Proclaim this among the nations:*
> *Prepare war,*
> *   stir up the warriors.*
> *Let all the soldiers draw near,*
> *   let them come up.*
> *Beat your plowshares into swords*
> *   and your pruning hooks into spears. . . ."*

Happy New Year indeed!

III

At that New Year's Eve party at midnight we watched on TV as the glittering ball descended on Times Square, we kissed our spouses and hugged our friends, we blew our horns and made noise with our noisemakers, we threw streamers over the rafters of the den where we greeted that particular new year.

"Happy New Year," we said to each other when midnight struck. Then we went back to eating and drinking and the private conversations we had interrupted to greet the new year.

I sat down beside the man whose stepson was suffering from depression, and we talked. He had no explanations; neither did I. We just talked about this young man and the behavior that had led to his hospitalization. Soon my wife caught my eye, signaling that we should be leaving. I got up and said, "I hope this year will be better for you than the last one."

And he said, "It's been a good year so far."

The new year was thirty-one minutes old, and he said, "It's been a good year so far." He made a joke, and I laughed.

If anything can save us from the fears and anxieties we all feel about a new year, it's humor. I think this couple and their son will make it because my friend could see something good and something to joke about, even at that dark hour.

Someone once said that if the problem for the believer is explaining how God can be good yet the world be full of evil, then the problem for the unbeliever is explaining how an evil world can be full of so much good. In the face of a wrenching personal crisis, under the shadow of ominous world events, my friend could say something funny. He could make a joke.

Where do people get the resources to cope with the pretty unhappy new year facing them? Where will you, where will I, get the resources to cope with our new year and all of its uncertainties and threats? In a world where good and evil are ambiguous, where they seem to be mixed in roughly equal parts, why should we believe in good and its ultimate triumph? Why should we live our lives with the faith that good will win out in the end?

IV

One of the ways the Bible answers that question is to give us an image—"the peaceable kingdom" as we have come to call it. This image is found in the book of Isaiah, where the prophet says a day will come when soldiers will beat their swords into plowshares and their spears into pruning hooks and natural enemies like the lion and the lamb will lie down in peace with each other.

This vision of Isaiah's was a vision of the future, a vision of the Day of the Lord, which was coming at some later moment in history. This vision was not true in Isaiah's day, nor was it true when the prophet Joel wrote his vicious parody of it four hundred years later. To many of us worldly-wise observers of the contemporary scene, it seems no truer today than it did then. Why should we, with all of our problems, be more ready to believe in a vision of a peaceable kingdom than Joel was in 400 B.C.? Is our world really any better than his—except that we have better and more sophisticated ways to kill ourselves? Why could my friend say something funny in the face of a new year that did not promise to be all that much fun for him?

The only difference I can think of between our times and the time of the prophet Joel is that Jesus Christ has come into the world and, in coming, has claimed to bring that peaceable kingdom with him. Jesus says, in the Gospel of Luke, that it is

God's good pleasure to give us the kingdom. It is God's pleasure to make that kingdom of peace real for us.

And in case we should mistakenly think that this peaceable kingdom is something that is going to happen some time in the future (as it was for Isaiah), a little later on Jesus says, "The kingdom of God is among you." The verb is in the present tense, not the future. The reign of God is a present reality we can experience now, not merely something we look for in a distant, far-off eschatological future.

It is the presence of that reign of God among us that enables us to look at the darkest future and make a joke, say something funny, at least smile. It is the presence of that kingdom of peace among us that enables us to be willing to give up everything for the sake of the kingdom. Paradoxically, giving up everything for the sake of God's rule is the way we get everything we need. And knowing this is the way to peace.

V

This peaceable kingdom within us is not to be understood as a good feeling we have about ourselves or our world. It may not be a good feeling at all. It is not to be understood as personal salvation while the world around us goes to hell. The kingdom of God within us is manifest rather in the confidence we have that no matter how bad we may feel or no matter how bad our circumstances get, God is seeing to it that things are turning out for the good. Not that things will turn out necessarily the way we want them to, but rather that whatever has gone wrong is being put right and that whatever happens—even if it's the worst we can imagine—is somehow being redeemed in God's goodness.

The peaceable kingdom of God within us is something else as well—it's the power within us to do good, to make some difference in our world for God. It is the belief that God works through us to extend this peaceable kingdom to others. It doesn't come with the guarantee that others will listen and respond with their own faith, hope, and courage. But it does come with the guarantee that God is in the work we do for this peaceable kingdom.

In the movie *The Godfather, Part III*, Don Corleone, the godfather, goes to Rome to work a business deal with the Vatican as a part of his never-ending yet always frustrated quest for respectability. He has an interview with Cardinal Lamberto, who asks him if he wants to make his confession. At first Don Corleone refuses, making a nervous little joke about how they don't have that much time. However, he needs this cardinal's help, so he haltingly confesses his marital infidelities and then the murder of his brother. On finally admitting this most heinous of his sins, he breaks down and begins to weep. Cardinal Lamberto pronounces the Latin words of absolution and then says, "I know you don't believe this, but you have been redeemed."

What the cardinal was saying is that even in a person like Don Corleone, the godfather/adulterer/murderer/fratricide, the peaceable kingdom of God can still become a reality. No matter our burden of fear or anger or hatred or anxiety; no matter what the world has done to us; no matter what we've done to the world— there is always the possibility that the peaceable kingdom can be ours; there is always the reality that nothing can keep us from this peaceable kingdom other than our own refusal to let it be.

You may not believe this, but you have been redeemed.

You may not believe this, but you are being redeemed.

You may not believe this, but you will be redeemed.

And because all this is true, you and I and everyone else who believes that the peaceable kingdom of God has come in Christ— we can really and truly say, "Happy New Year!"

The Miracles of Jesus

Healings Then and Now

Matthew 8:1-17

I

Matthew is generally considered the most "Jewish" of the four Gospels. That is, Matthew seems to have closer affinities with Judaism than the other Gospels and quite consciously attempts to show that Jesus fulfills the Jewish law in every important way. Scholars also believe that the church for which this Gospel was written was probably a congregation with a significant population of Jewish Christians.

One reason for believing this is the way the Gospel is organized into five books or divisions, apparently patterned after the five books of Moses, the Torah. Matthew's five books are bracketed by the birth and temptation narratives of chapters 1-4 and the passion narrative of chapters 26-28. The first book of Matthew's "Torah" is the Sermon on the Mount, which parallels Moses' receiving the Law on Mount Sinai. In the same way Moses went up onto a mountain to receive God's teaching, so Jesus goes up onto a mountain to give God's teaching. The Sermon on the Mount is, among other things, a running commentary on the Mosaic law, with Jesus' teaching being compared more than favorably with the Law of Moses: "You have heard it said by those of old . . . but I say unto you. . . ." Jesus never rejects the Mosaic law, but Matthew does present him as going beyond it, elevating it, giving it a deeper significance.

The second of Matthew's books begins in chapter 8 with a series of healings. In the same way that the Sermon on the Mount makes a running comparison and contrast between Jesus' teaching and the Mosaic law, so the second of Matthew's books will imply a comparison and contrast between the person of Jesus and that of Moses.

Before examining the actual healing stories, however, we need to note two important aspects of miracle stories that affect our understanding of them. The first has to do with the general nature of the Gospels. None of the Gospels was written to give us the literal details of Jesus' ministry. None of them is a biography in our sense of the word. Instead, they were written to make a theological statement about Jesus. Consequently, the evangelists took events from Jesus' life and rearranged them for theological purposes. What they did is analogous to what a film editor does in taking raw film footage and splicing the pieces together to make a movie. In Matthew we find blocks of material put together to teach theological, not historical, truth. (This is not to say that the Gospels don't contain historical material, but only to emphasize that their primary purpose is theological.) This comment about the general nature of the Gospels applies to the miracle stories. In studying them, we primarily want to discover what they teach us about Jesus. The miracle stories, in other words, are revelatory narratives. They are told to reveal something to us about Jesus and our relation to him.

The second aspect we need to note is that the miracle stories are stories of redemption or salvation. When Jesus performed a miracle—whether a healing or nature miracle—his purpose was to deliver someone from harmful, debilitating, or threatening circumstances. He didn't do miracles to show off or to curry favor or to create a popular following. His miracles were acts of compassion for the purpose of salvation. In fact, Jesus was apparently bothered by the popular reaction to his miracles. The crowds, apparently, focused on the power manifested in the miracles rather than on their purpose. Consequently, Jesus on occasion sought to escape from the crowds because of their misunderstanding.

II

The first of Jesus' miracles recorded in Matthew is the healing of a leper. Jesus has just come down off the mountain, having finished his Sermon on the Mount. "Great crowds," Matthew says, follow him, presumably the crowd who had just listened to his teaching. A leper greets Jesus at the bottom of the mountain and says, "Lord, if you choose, you can make me clean." Jesus reaches out, touches the man kneeling in front of him, and says,

"I do choose. Be made clean!" (Matthew 8:2-3). The leprosy immediately disappears. Jesus commands the man to fulfill the obligations of the Mosaic law and receive certification from a priest that he has been cured. Jesus also commands him to remain silent about how he was cured.

In this terse narrative there are two important details that continue the comparison and contrast between Jesus and Moses. The first is that the leper kneels in front of Jesus—a recognition of Jesus' power and authority and also an act of worship. No one would have knelt before Moses, that is, worshiped him. The leper's act says that he recognizes that one greater than Moses is here. This astounding and unprecedented act of the leper is paralleled by an astounding and unprecedented act of Jesus. Upon hearing the man's request, with its acknowledgment of his power to heal, Jesus reaches out and touches the leper, an act forbidden by the Law of Moses. Lepers were unclean. To touch one meant to become unclean and to become separated from the rest of the community. Yet, Jesus deliberately touches him. Jesus runs the risk of ostracism in order to heal this outcast and restore him to his community.

We do not know what happened to this cleansed leper—at least Matthew doesn't tell us, because Matthew's interest is not in the miracle itself, but rather in what the miracle says about Jesus. This is why the Gospel immediately goes on to the next miracle, the healing of the Roman centurion's servant. (Mark does tell us that the leper disobeys Jesus and tells everyone that Jesus cured him. Mark is silent about whether or not the man goes to a priest for certification. If not, he was doubly disobedient.)

III

As Jesus enters Capernaum, a Roman soldier, identified only as a centurion, comes up to him with a request for help. A servant of his, a boy, is lying "at home paralyzed and racked with pain." There must be something in the centurion's statement that touches Jesus deeply, for his response is that he will immediately come to the centurion's house and cure the boy. It is significant that the soldier himself has come to Jesus with his request, especially in light of what he subsequently says about authority and command. A centurion, after all, has a lot of responsibility. A hundred Roman soldiers are under his command. He is responsible both for them and to them. The centurions were, in fact, the backbone of the Roman army. Yet this centurion takes his own very valuable time to make a personal appeal to Jesus for help. He could have sent someone else instead but chooses to come in person. The centurion's act is all the more remarkable because it is a servant who commands his time. The Roman high command, I suspect, would look askance at a centurion taking time off the job for a mere servant.

Perhaps it is for these reasons that Jesus says he will come to cure the boy before the centurion even has a chance to make a formal request. Perhaps Jesus is responding to the compassion for suffering this man evidences; he says the boy "is racked with pain," and there seems to be pain in the man's words. Whatever the reason, the centurion now shows even more remarkable character in his response to Jesus' response. "I'm not asking you to come to my house," he says. "I'm not worthy to have you under my roof. All I'm asking is that you say words of healing. That will be enough, because I understand authority and I understand that a word from the proper authority is sufficient. All I'm asking is that you speak the words of healing, and it will be done, because you have the authority to make such a command."

If this man has great compassion, then he has even greater faith. Presumably he has never met Jesus, yet he is willing to trust this stranger with the well-being of a person who is obviously important to him. Jesus' comment expresses in the highest terms possible the quality of this man's faith. A Gentile—worse, a Roman; worse, a Roman soldier—has faith greater than any person Jesus found in Israel. (And this man's faith becomes the occasion of a saying of Jesus to the effect that the kingdom of God will be populated by a lot of surprising people. Immigrants will be the real citizens of this kingdom, not the natives.)

Jesus then demonstrates the truth of the centurion's comment about the power and authority of words when he speaks a word of healing and assures this Gentile, this Roman, this soldier that his servant will get well. "At that moment," Matthew says, "the boy recovered."

IV

This miracle of the healing of the centurion's servant—the longest of those recorded in Matthew 8—is followed immediately by the shortest, the healing of Peter's mother-in-law. Although Matthew doesn't say so directly, he implies that when Jesus finished the Sermon on the Mount, he and the disciples set out for Peter's house in Capernaum. These first two miracles of healing, therefore, occurred on the way to the house where they were to stay. If this is so, then Peter probably had sent word ahead that they were coming so his mother-in-law could prepare to greet them and show the hospitality expected of her. However, when Jesus and his disciples get to Peter's house, they find his mother-in-law in bed with a fever. Luke calls it a high fever, implying that it is life-threatening. Matthew indicates the seriousness of the fever by saying she was in bed; that is, she was incapacitated. The fever threatens this woman's life, but it also threatens her social standing. Hospitality is a serious matter in the Near East, and failure to show hospitality is a serious breach of expected conduct. This illness throws everything into confusion. If Peter cannot provide the hospitality he promised, where will they all stay, and who will provide them with food and a place to rest?

In Mark and Luke, Jesus is told about the problem with an implicit request that he do something about it. But in Matthew's account no one says anything. Matthew says that Jesus "went to Peter's house and found Peter's mother-in-law in bed with fever. So he took her by the hand; the fever left her, and she got up and waited on him." In Matthew, Jesus doesn't have to be told about the problem. He intuitively understands the situation with all of its ramifications and acts to bring healing, to set a confused and upsetting situation aright.

We can now see a general pattern to the miracles in Matthew. There is, first, a problem: a leper wanting to be clean, a paralyzed boy racked with pain, a hostess so ill she cannot perform her duties of hospitality. There is, second, a request for help, at least implicit in the situation: the leper states what he wants explicitly, as does the centurion, and though no one says anything in the story of Peter's mother-in-law, the need is obvious. Third, Jesus responds either in word or deed or both: he stretches out his hand to touch the leper and says words of healing; he tells the centurion he will come with him and then speaks words of healing; he goes straight to Peter's mother-in-law and takes her by the hand (but says nothing). Jesus' response in word and deed then leads to the miracle itself: the leper's disease is cured immediately; the centurion's servant recovers the moment Jesus pronounces the words of healing; Peter's mother-in-law's fever breaks when Jesus takes her by the hand. The final element is the result the miracle brings about, though Matthew doesn't state what that result is in the first two cases but only in the third: as a result of the healing, Peter's mother-in-law is able to get up and wait on Jesus. We can assume that as a result of the leper's healing, he was restored to family and friends; and as a result of the servant's healing, he was restored to the service of the centurion.

V

What do these stories reveal? What do they teach us about Jesus? Matthew has a specific purpose in mind, which he tells us at the end of this section in verses 16 and 17. These verses summarize Jesus' healing activities, then quote Isaiah 53:4: "He took away our illnesses and lifted our diseases from us." This quotation comes from one of the Suffering Servant songs, which means it is a messianic prophecy. One of the signs that the messianic age has begun is the kind of healings Jesus performs. Jesus must, therefore, be the Messiah. Jesus is the one for whom the Jews have been looking; Jesus is the Christ.

These healings reveal that Jesus is the Messiah, the Savior prophesied by the great Hebrew prophets. But they also reveal something of the nature of the salvation this Savior brings. After Jesus heals the leper, he commands the man to fulfill the obligations of the law concerning the cure of leprosy. Why does Jesus do this? Isn't the physical healing sufficient? The answer is that Jesus is concerned with more than just physical health. The man's disease has done more than decimate his body; it has also ruined his relations with others because as a leper he is cut off from his community; he is ostracized. His healing restores not only his health but also his social standing. This is the reason for the priestly certification—to announce to his community that he is fully restored to his rightful position in the social order. Similarly, the healing of the centurion's servant obviously makes it possible for him to serve his master once more. And the healing of Peter's mother-in-law enables her to fulfill her proper role in society as the hostess, the one who extends hospitality to the traveler and the stranger. The kind of salvation Jesus brings is salvation for the whole person in all aspects of one's personhood.

The healings of Jesus also give us a standard by which to judge claims of healing today. Christians have practiced healing since the days of the apostles, and we must never assume that healing today is impossible. The power of God at work in Jesus' healing has not changed; God still has the power to create and recreate the natural order. So we should continue to pray for the sick, that God will heal them. But we should also keep in mind that Jesus used his healing powers for the benefit of others and not for his own advancement. In fact, he tried to avoid the popular misunderstanding of his powers that would have turned him into some kind of magician or the leader of a cult. The standard for judging healing claims today is, therefore, twofold. First, does the healing practice focus on all the needs of the sick person and on the way physical health is interrelated with social and spiritual well-being? Second (this is a negative standard), does the healing practice call attention to the healer, and is it used to advance the healer's own interests? Does it, for example, make the healer wealthy and powerful?

We should be suspicious of contemporary faith healers who don't measure up to these standards.

Good News/Bad News from the Mouths of Demons

Matthew 8:18-34

I

In dealing with the first three miracles in Matthew 8, we noted the following: Matthew is the most Jewish of all the Gospels, presenting Jesus as the new Moses, whose power and authority exceed even that of the first Moses. Matthew groups the material in this Gospel for theological reasons and is not really concerned to give us an exact chronology of Jesus' life. That is, Matthew is usually concerned to make a theological point rather than to write objective history. There is also a repeated pattern in the healing stories: presentation of the problem, request for help (sometimes implied, not stated), Jesus' response in word or deed or both, the miracle itself resolving the problem and eliminating the threat, and then the result for the one healed (again sometimes implied rather than stated). These stories of healings are salvation stories—that is, they restore the afflicted ones to both bodily health and full human community and, thus, to full personhood. The leper, the centurion's servant, and Peter's mother-in-law can once again function as full members of their communities.

The first of the two miracles in Matthew 8:18-34 is the first of the nature miracles Matthew records. In this miracle Jesus calms a storm, thereby demonstrating his lordship over nature. But we will misunderstand this story if we fail to set it in the context Matthew provides for it. That context is a discussion of Christian discipleship.

After Jesus cured Peter's mother-in-law, the word must have

spread quickly through Capernaum that Jesus had miraculous powers, with the consequence that "many who were possessed with devils" and many who were sick came to Jesus, and he healed them. The situation, however, was threatening to get out of hand, so in verse 18 Matthew says that when Jesus saw the crowds "surrounding him" he decided to cross over the Sea of Galilee to escape them. The danger Jesus perceived in this popular outpouring was that of popular misunderstanding. Jesus could have quite easily been trapped by the image of "wonder worker" or "magician" or "revolutionary." So, he decides to defuse this situation by leaving and letting this popular enthusiasm, which is headed in the wrong direction, die down.

II

But before he can get into the boat to cross the Sea of Galilee, he is stopped—twice. And both of these interruptions concern the question of discipleship. A doctor of the Law comes up and vows to follow Jesus wherever he goes. He probably means this quite literally, that he is prepared to traipse all over Galilee with Jesus. But on a deeper level, of course, he means that he wants to be Jesus' disciple, that he wants to accept Jesus' teaching and try to follow it as he lives his life. Jesus, headed for the boat, stops to deal with this would-be disciple. His response is, in effect, to ask this doctor of the Law a question. "Do you know what you're asking? You're a doctor of the Law, and as such you have status, authority, and power. If you follow me, either literally or on the deeper level of living by my teaching, you'll have to be ready to give all that up. In fact, the beasts of the field have more security than you will have as my disciple. They at least know where they will sleep each night. If you become my disciple, you won't even be sure of that. Are you sure you understand the cost of being my disciple?"

This is the point Matthew wants to make in telling this story. Having made it, he doesn't even tell us what this learned man says or does in response to Jesus. Instead, Matthew immediately goes on to the second interruption. Jesus starts toward the boat again, but another man stops him, vowing his discipleship. Presumably he has heard Jesus' response to the doctor of the Law and is saying he is willing to accept such insecurity. But his avowal of discipleship comes with a request—a reasonable, personal, humane request. "Let me first bury my father," he says. What he means is that his father is an old man who will die soon. As a son, this man's highest obligation is to take care of his father until death and then see to a proper burial. Clearly, becoming a disciple now would make this duty difficult to carry out. This request for a delay is in every way reasonable.

Unfortunately there is something that is unreasonable about following Jesus. Discipleship, Jesus says in response, may unfortunately be inconvenient for our merely human obligations. "Let the dead bury their dead," Jesus says. What he means is that we cannot become disciples with strings attached or with prior conditions or with our fingers crossed. In other relations, perhaps, we can bargain and negotiate and jockey for position, but not in our relationship with Christ. We either follow Christ or we don't. We either are his disciples or we're not. Once again, Matthew's concern is simply to make this point about the cost of discipleship rather than to tell us what happened. We don't know what this man decided, though the implication in both these cases is that these two men did not follow Jesus; discipleship was too costly for them.

III

Does anyone follow Jesus? Yes, because the very next verse says that Jesus "got into the boat, and his disciples followed him." The delay occasioned by the interviews with these would-be disciples is important on a literal level because it allows time for the weather to change. Had Jesus gone directly to the boat, he and his disciples might have stayed ahead of the storm and escaped the danger which, in fact, befell them. While Jesus talked with these two men, however, the weather began to change, and anyone experienced in such matters would know that now is not the time to take a boat out onto the Sea of Galilee. Jesus' disciples are experienced in such matters. Some of them have spent their whole adult lives fishing this body of water. They know it is dangerous to follow Jesus into the boat. But, Matthew says, "His disciples followed him."

The act of getting into the boat with Jesus is an act of discipleship that perfectly illustrates what Jesus has been teaching about the risks and insecurities of following him. The two men who stopped Jesus on the way to the boat were not ready to take these risks, and so they are not disciples. True disciples are ready to follow Jesus onto dangerous waters. True disciples are ready to accept the dangers and uncertainties of discipleship. No sooner is the boat well under way than the storm breaks. Matthew calls it a "great storm," meaning that it is dangerous and threatens to swamp the boat. The "waves were breaking right over the boat," he writes. The disciples draw on all their skill and experience to keep the boat afloat, but to no avail. Finally, in desperation, they call to Jesus, who is asleep in the stern. "Save us, Lord!" they cry.

It is interesting that the storm doesn't seem to disturb Jesus' sleep, but the desperate cries of the disciples do. He awakens and immediately grasps the situation. He rebukes his disciples with stern words: "Why are you such cowards? How little faith you have!" The disciples have enough faith to have followed Jesus, but they still do not understand the full implications of who he is. They still do not know that when they are with him, when they are in his presence, there is no storm, no matter how great, that can harm them. Jesus' rebuke, though harsh, is born out of frustrated love. He is saying in effect, "You still don't know who I am."

Then, Jesus does something dramatic. In the midst of this raging storm, with waves breaking over the boat, with the boat pitching and yawing wildly, he stands up. The disciples exemplify fear. Jesus exemplifies calm courage. He stands up and rebukes the wind and the sea. "And there was a dead calm." There are two storms here—the storm of the disciples' fear and the storm on the Sea of Galilee. Jesus rebukes both and calms both. The disciples are "astonished" at Jesus' action and ask, "What sort of man is this? Even the wind and the sea obey him." Their amazement simply underscores their lack of understanding. If they had known what sort of man this is, they would not have been fearful.

IV

Very early in the history of Christianity the boat became a symbol for the church. The church was understood as an "ark of salvation," carrying believers safely over the flood that destroys everything else. This story of the calming of the storm, therefore, becomes a parable of Christian discipleship. It becomes a model of what to expect if you become a Christian, if you identify your life with the church. You can expect storms. You can expect to be buffeted and tossed around by a hostile world. You can expect danger, uncertainty, risk, opposition. You had better even be prepared to accept persecution. If this is what discipleship means, then why become a disciple? Doesn't the world buffet us enough already? Why make it worse by following Christ?

Matthew's answer is found in the cry of the disciples at the height of the storm: "Save us, Lord; we are sinking!" This is the cry of all who come into the church, and this is why we come to Christ—for salvation. "Save us, Lord." All who come to Christ do so because they believe Christ can save them from everything that threatens them. This cry has a liturgical ring to it. It may represent one element of Christian worship in the late first century. In any case, it represents the fundamental question for the church. Is Christ really the one who can save? Or will he prove to be yet another false messiah? Is the church's proclamation truly Good News, so that if you believe it you will indeed be saved? Or is it bad news, one more false claim, one more cruel joke played on desperate people?

The point of the miracle is to answer this question. In the same way that Jesus was not "present" in the storm (he was asleep), so he is no longer present in the church. But he is the Messiah, and he is the Lord. When he was physically present in the world, he calmed a literal storm on the Sea of Galilee and saved a literal boatful of disciples. He is still present, though not physically, and he can therefore still save his disciples from whatever storms threaten them. When Jesus awakens in response to the disciples' frantic cries, he demonstrates what the church proclaims is true: He is the one from God; he is the Lord; he is the one through whom we may be saved, if only we have faith, if only we are willing to follow him. That is why Jesus addresses his disciples before he addresses the storm. The real problem isn't the storm. The real problem is the disciples' weak faith and their fear, which threatens to overwhelm that faith. The most important thing is that they recognize his power to save and that they believe in him. This, of course, is the greatest danger the church faces in any generation. Do we really trust in Jesus to save us, or do we really trust in something or someone else?

"What manner of man is this?" the disciples ask, shaking their heads in wonder. That is the question for all of us, and the answer is: Jesus is the Son of God, the Savior. The storm is an evil power that Jesus subdues by his word alone. Jesus is the ruler of a kingdom in which even natural forces are subservient to his commands. This great storm is followed by a great calm—so great is Jesus' power.

V

In case we miss the implicit answer to the most fundamental question raised by the calming of the storm, Matthew makes it explicit in the sequel—the healing of the Gadarene demoniacs. When the boat that has weathered this great storm lands, its occupants are met by yet a third kind of storm—the storm of emotional and mental derangement. Two demon-possessed men, who live along the shore in caves that serve as tombs for the people of Gadara, see Jesus and the disciples land and rush from their hiding place to scare them off. These tombs, well outside the town (since death and corpses defile), are an appropriate dwelling place for these wild men possessed of evil spirits. They are the living dead, alive only in a physical sense, hardly human at all, cut off as they are from all meaningful contact with others.

They surely must have presented a terrifying aspect—dirty, ragged, unkempt, shouting obscene and blasphemous phrases. Today we would call them the criminally insane. Matthew says they are "violent"—so much so that "no one dared pass that way." Except Jesus, who happens to land on their turf. They rush out of their caves, down the hillside, yelling and screaming, a technique that has proved terrifyingly effective so far in scaring people off. "You son of God, what do you want with us?" they scream. "Have you come here to torment us before our time?" How full of suffering and sorrow their cry is. All they have received from others, at least since the onset of their dementia, is torment. By fleeing to a place where no one will dare to bother them and creating their own little society of outcasts, they have found temporary relief from their torment. But it is only temporary. They believe their ultimate fate will be unending pain and suffering. There is no cure, they believe, for what ails them. And what ails them can only get worse. They can't imagine that Jesus, the Son of God, can have any other intention than to torment them. Perhaps Jesus is even more threatening to them than ordinary people because, as Son of God, he will have greater power to torment. Their fear of Jesus is worsened because they believe they still have some time left before madness completely overtakes them. "Have you come here to torment us before our time?" they ask. Have you come to take away even this brief respite?

The demoniacs are more perceptive than Jesus' disciples. In fact, they answer the disciples' question "What sort of man is this?" when they address Jesus as the "Son of God." Their address to Jesus is also the answer to the question that the church's proclamation of the Gospel raises. Is Jesus the Son of God? Is Jesus the Savior? The demons pronounce the Good News—yes, Jesus is the Son of God. And that means that Jesus comes not to torment, but to save. Jesus' compassion extends even to the demons. "If you drive us out," they beg, "send us into that herd of pigs." The demons, destined for hell, beg for a little mercy, for a delay in their return to torment. And Jesus grants them their request. The demons possess the pigs, who go mad, rush over the edge of the bluff into the sea and drown.

In these miracles Jesus demonstrates his power and authority over nature, over human nature, and even over the realm of spirits. Surely there can be no doubt now that he is the Son of God, the Savior. And surely, now, everyone who has witnessed his saving power will believe in him and become his disciple. Matthew, however, gives this parable of discipleship one more twist, which illustrates how difficult and costly this discipleship is. The herdsmen in charge of the swine take to their heels back to the town and tell everyone what has happened, including (Matthew is careful to note) the healing of the two madmen, who had once been members of their community, who had once been among their friends. The whole town comes out to the tombs where this miracle has happened. Are they coming in gratitude for Jesus' restoration of two of their community? No, they beg Jesus to leave. The people of Gadara want nothing to do with a Savior who threatens to overturn their economic security, who values persons above pigs. They want nothing to do with a Savior who demonstrates such awesome power and authority. If they allow such a one to stay around very long, he will start changing things, he will confront them with the question of discipleship. That would be too upsetting. Life is difficult enough as it is (after all, they have been reduced to herding swine for their livelihood). They beg Jesus to leave because discipleship for them is too costly.

A Privileged President and a Marginalized Woman

Matthew 9:18-26; Mark 5:21-43

I

The healings of the woman with the flow of blood and Jairus's daughter are recorded in parallel passages in Matthew and Mark; and of the two accounts, Mark's is the more elaborate, dramatic, and interesting. We will mention Matthew's but concentrate on Mark's.

In Matthew's version Jesus is sitting "at table" in Matthew's house answering questions that his ministry and teaching have raised. Why, for example, does he consort with "many bad characters" (like Matthew, the tax collector) instead of associating with the righteous? Jesus points out to the Pharisees (who ask this question) that it's sinners who need what he has to offer, so how can they get what he has to offer if he refuses to associate with them? The Pharisees' question is a hostile one, as we would expect from representatives of a group with whom Jesus engaged in a continuous verbal battle. But disciples of John the Baptist are also there, and they too are bothered by Jesus' willingness to be the guest at parties of which the ascetic John the Baptist would never approve. John, long on self-denial but short on pleasure, would not approve the general socializing Jesus seems to have done.

Jesus' answer to John's disciples is a reprimand. People shouldn't mourn when the bridegroom is still with them and it's still possible to feast, Jesus says. People don't put new cloth in old worn clothing or new wine in old, rotting wineskins. If you do that, you lose both the garment and the new cloth, the wine and the wineskin. This is a new age Jesus is bringing in, and this new age demands new ways of doing things. John's asceticism is appropriate for John. But the reign of God Jesus brings is of a different order.

While he is in the very act of making these pronouncements, the president of the synagogue comes up to make a formal request. "My daughter has just died," he says, bowing low, "but come and lay your hand on her and she will live." Without saying a word, Jesus gets up from the table and follows this man. But they don't get far before an interruption occurs. A woman who for twelve years has suffered from a hemorrhage comes up behind Jesus and touches the edge of Jesus' cloak, believing that action will be sufficient to heal her. The touch does not cure, but it does get Jesus' attention. He stops, faces the woman, and says, "Take heart, my daughter, your faith has cured you." At that moment, Matthew says, when Jesus speaks these words, the woman is healed.

When Jesus and the president of the synagogue finally arrive at the house, they find all the activity that death causes. Matthew calls it a "general commotion." Jesus commands the crowd to be off, then explains the reason for this breach of death's etiquette. "The girl is not dead," he says, "she is asleep." The crowd just laughs (they know death when they see it), but Jesus turns them out all the same. Going into the death chamber, he takes the girl by the hand, and she rises from the bed, alive and well.

II

That's Matthew's version. Mark's account places these miracles in a different context. In Mark, Jesus has just returned from curing the Gerasene demoniac, whose fellow townspeople had ordered Jesus to leave because of the unfortunate incident with the pigs. When Jesus steps out of the boat, a great crowd is waiting for him. Out of this crowd, the president of one of the synagogues comes up (Mark tells us his name is Jairus) and falls on his knees before Jesus with a request full of anguish: "My little daughter is at death's door. I beg you to come and lay your hands on her to cure her and save her life." Unlike Matthew's very formal and correct Jewish official, this Jairus is hurting and desperate. He—a ruler of the synagogue, one of the most important men in the town—is reduced to begging. Without saying a word, Jesus goes with Jairus, and the "great crowd" that greeted Jesus follows him to see what will happen.

Mark emphasizes the size and unruliness of this crowd in order to make the interruption by the hemorrhaging woman all that more remarkable. We must imagine the crowd pressing around Jesus, jostling him, in much the same way crowds today push and shove to get closer to media stars or popular politicians. As all of this jostling goes on, the woman comes up from behind simply to touch Jesus' outer garment, believing that action may be sufficient to heal her. Mark emphasizes this woman's suffering. There is, of course, the physical suffering, but there is also the suffering caused by the medical treatment, which not only has not helped but has actually worsened her condition. Her approach to Jesus speaks volumes about her condition. She dare not confront Jesus face to face with her need. Instead, she hopes that he can heal without his knowing it. What better opportunity than this, with the crowd pressing all around!

Jairus and this anonymous woman are very different in social standing, power, and influence; yet they are alike in their desperate need for help and in their belief that Jesus is their last hope. Jairus's daughter is at "death's door," implying that she has been ill for some time and has gradually worsened until now it's clear she is going to die. Jairus has undoubtedly done everything he could to save his daughter. (Has he brought in some of the same physicians who treated the woman to no avail?) Now both of these very different people are united in their common need and their common belief that only Jesus can help.

They are also united in their readiness to act. Jesus had been in this area just a short while before, teaching and performing miracles. Both Jairus and this anonymous woman must have heard about Jesus; so when he returned, both were ready to act. Perhaps the woman had thought about approaching Jesus before but lacked the courage. Perhaps Jairus's daughter had not been as ill as she was now, so Jairus hadn't needed a miracle worker then. But now the woman has a second chance and is determined not to lose it, and Jairus needs more than human help, since all human help has been exhausted.

III

There is an urgency about Jairus's request. His daughter is about to die; and if Jesus doesn't get there soon, it will be too late. At this point Jairus does not believe that Jesus can do more than cure the sick. Death is a limit beyond which not even Jesus can go. There must be no delay. But there is a delay! The unnamed woman with the hemorrhage touches Jesus' cloak, and this mere touching is sufficient to heal her. Her plan is, therefore, partly successful. She thought this act would heal her (and it did), and she also thought it would preserve her anonymity (but it didn't). Why does she desire to remain anonymous? Because she sees herself as an insignificant person who could never ask Jesus for help face to face. She could never do what Jairus has done. Jairus is a man whose social standing has guaranteed preference and privilege for him all of his life so that he expects his requests to be granted. Jairus, though desperate, betrays the confidence of the privileged. The woman, also desperate, betrays the diffidence of the marginal.

Jesus stops, and both Jairus and the woman wish he hadn't. Jesus stops because he knows that healing power has gone out of him. He knows that someone else has needed his help. So he stops and asks what can only appear to be a silly question. "Who touched my clothes?" The disciples can't believe what is happening. Here he is, racing against time to help this Very Important Person, with this mob pushing and shoving all around him, and he stops to ask who touched him. The crowd must also be buzzing with similar questions.

What follows is a wonderful scene of compassion. Jesus scans the crowd trying to identify the person who needed his healing power but was afraid to ask. The woman, trembling with fear, finally comes forward. She knows she's been healed, so why is she trembling? Part of the answer is that all of her life she has been on the margin of her community (or at least for the last twelve years she has), and now she is asked to move to the very center of attention. In addition, she has interrupted this important journey, which allowed no delays. She has, furthermore, endangered Jesus' mission by touching him. She is unclean, and her touch defiles Jesus. How can a ritually unclean rabbi work a miracle? But Mark gives another reason for her fear—"she grasped what had happened to her." For twelve years she had been hoping and praying for healing, and now her prayers had been answered. It is a fearful thing to have your prayers answered. In this state of mind, she identifies herself, falls at Jesus' feet (just as Jairus had done), and tells her story, which eats up precious minutes. But Jesus listens, his full attention on this nameless woman who has been an outcast for at least twelve years. When she finishes, Jesus pronounces a benediction in tender, compassionate terms: "My daughter, your faith has cured you. Go in peace, free forever from this trouble."

IV

What a wonderful yet disturbing scene this is. Jesus turns all our values upside down. From a strictly utilitarian point of view, this healing could have been delayed. This woman's life was not threatened, not like Jairus's daughter. Yet Jesus stops to minister to her. And as a result, Jairus's worst fears are realized. While Jesus talks with this woman, a messenger comes up with bad news, whispering in Jairus's ear, "Don't trouble the rabbi any more, your daughter is dead." Jesus might have cured a sick child, but not even he can do something for a dead child. Jesus, however, knows what has happened and, turning from the woman to Jairus, says, "Don't be afraid, just have faith." Jairus—ruler of the synagogue, a man of position, prestige, and power, the religious leader of his community—should follow the example of an unclean, outcast woman, a marginal member of the society of which Jairus is a privileged member. This very unlikely person is a model of faith for this religious leader.

When they reach the house, the scene is one of noise and lament, a "great commotion." There is weeping and wailing and gnashing of teeth—all of the actions of the professional mourner. Why such confusion? For ancient people, death represented the reascendance of the forces of chaos that God had subdued in the act of creation. In death, chaos takes its revenge and reasserts itself. The tumult of the mourners expresses this fear of chaos and its power to destroy order, well-being, and life. The kind of mourning Jesus witnesses at Jairus's' house implies the belief that death is final, the last word about us. Jesus' question, "Why this crying and commotion?" is a questioning of this belief in death's power. And in case we miss his point, Jesus goes on to say, "The child is not dead: she is asleep."

This crowd, as in Matthew's account, laughs. So, Jesus puts them out, dismisses them. Now they know he's serious, and his action causes them great concern. They are professional mourners who are paid to weep and wail and gnash their teeth. Jesus' dismissal means they won't be paid, they've been fired. This is not a politic thing for Jesus to do. Nevertheless, he does it anyway, then enters the death chamber, allowing only the girl's parents and three of his disciples (Peter, James, and John) to enter with him. He takes the child by the hand and says, "Get up, my child." And she does. All of the adults (except Jesus) are amazed. Perhaps the little girl is too (though we don't know what her reaction was). Jesus then commands Jairus not to tell anyone what has happened and to give his daughter something to eat. This command to feed the child, which closes the narrative, is a nice touch. While the parents and the disciples stand around gawking in amazement, Jesus reminds them that the child has not eaten for some time and is therefore hungry. Even in these most wonderful of circumstances, Jesus doesn't lose sight of immediate need. It also emphasizes the completeness of her cure. She can eat like the healthy child she is now.

V

The setting for these two miracles was the controversy concerning Jesus' unorthodox behavior. He was criticized by the Pharisees because he freely consorted with sinners and seemed unconcerned with their failure to live up to the demands of the law. John the Baptist's disciples didn't object so much to the sinners as they did to the fact that Jesus apparently enjoyed their company and had a good time with them. Jesus socialized with sinners, and John's disciples would have preferred for Jesus merely to preach at them. To both sets of critics Jesus said, in effect, "I represent a new age in God's dealings with sinners. What may have been appropriate for you is not appropriate for my disciples. God is doing something new through me. Don't be so wedded to the past that you miss this new thing."

These two miracles we have just examined reinforce this teaching. They illustrate the way Jesus turns our values upside down. Both miracles have to do with women, who in Jesus' day were not considered to be equal to men as human beings. Women were relegated to an inferior social and economic status. They were among the marginalized people of their day. Yet when Jairus comes, Jesus immediately gets up to go with him to heal his daughter. And when the hemorrhaging woman touches his outer garment, he stops to learn her identity, hear her story, and bless her. Jesus responds to the need of a woman as readily and willingly as to that of a man. Implicit in his action in these miracles is a view that would do away with the prevailing view of his day. "Women are equal to men in importance," Jesus is saying. "Anyone who wants to be my disciple will not make value discriminations among people based on sexual differences."

Lest we think that Jesus' concern for Jairus's daughter grows out of Jairus's social status, we only need to reflect on the second miracle, which interrupts the progress of the first. Here the conflict resides in the claims of members of two different social and economic classes—the class of the privileged and the class of the marginalized or oppressed. When forced to choose, Jesus opted for the oppressed. This unnamed woman gets his full attention and his full compassion. Is Jesus trying to tell Jairus (and us) something? Is Jesus trying to tell Jairus (and us) that exalted standing in a community does not give anyone priority over the less exalted when there is a clash of needs and a conflict of resources?

And there's something else in these two miracles, something we've already seen in other miracle stories. These healings show Jesus as the giver of life—in all of its wholeness and completeness. Mark tells us something Matthew omits—that Jairus's daughter was twelve years old. Her death is particularly poignant because twelve is the traditional age in Judaism when a child comes to be considered an adult. At the very moment she should be entering into the best part of life, it is snatched from her. Jesus' raising her from the dead is more than a mere restoration of biological existence. It is a restoration to her full human potential. The miracle of Jairus's daughter is a miracle of redemption and salvation—her salvation being nothing less than being given back her chance for full human existence.

But the miracle of the hemorrhaging woman is also a resurrection story, a story of redemption from death. For twelve years this woman has been unable to live a fully human life. (Is Mark consciously linking these two women by the use of "twelve years"?) Her affliction cuts her off from the thing she most needs to become a whole human being—social intercourse with others. Jesus gives her back her life in its fullest sense just as much as he gives Jairus's daughter her life back in the literal sense. Jesus' benediction over this woman is that she can now "go in peace, free for ever from this trouble." The Jewish idea of peace is the idea of wholeness or completeness (rather than absence of conflict). Jesus' healing makes peace in this sense a possibility for her.

Once again we see that the primary point of a miracle story is to teach theology. These miracles show Jesus to be the Savior and Redeemer. That is, they show that Jesus is one who can give us life in all of its fullness, completeness, and abundance. The only requirement for receiving this life is faith, trust in Jesus, willingness to believe in him. Salvation is free to all who have faith, regardless of their standing in society.

The Feeding of the Five Thousand

Matthew 14:13-21; Mark 6:30-44

I

The feeding of the five thousand is one of the few stories found in all four of the Gospels. In fact, some scholars believe this story is actually told six times instead of four because they believe the feeding of the 4,000 is really another version of the same event (Matthew 15:29-39; Mark 8:1-10). We won't try to solve that problem here. But the fact that all four Gospels record this event and that Matthew and Mark also record another event that is similar (if not the same) in many ways to it indicates that this miracle of Jesus was extremely significant to the first Christians. Somehow this story captured the meaning of Christ in such a profound way that it was widely circulated among first-century Christians in a way other stories were not. There can be little doubt that in this miracle we have the essence of what Christ meant to the early church.

Our wealth of resources in some ways makes it difficult to deal with this story. Which of the four accounts should we use? Mark's is the fullest, with greater detail than the others. Yet the others all contribute unique elements that add to the richness of this story. I propose, therefore, that we follow the pattern I used in dealing with the story of Jairus's daughter and the hemorrhaging woman. I'll summarize the miracle as Matthew narrates it, then turn to Mark's fuller account to fill out the details, also drawing on Luke (and even John) where appropriate.

Matthew's account begins with the statement "When he heard what had happened Jesus withdrew privately by boat to a lonely place." The event that causes Jesus to withdraw to a lonely place is the murder of John the Baptist. Matthew has just narrated this story (14:1-12), and it is given as the reason for Jesus' actions. In other words, Jesus needs to think through the implications of John's murder. It is also, of course, a time to be careful. If Herod is in the mood to cut off heads, his next victim might very well be Jesus, who had had some association with John. The setting for this miracle in Matthew is, therefore, one of potential danger. What will Herod's next move be? But it is also a time of self-evaluation for Jesus. Does proclaiming the reign of God inevitably mean conflict with the powers that be? What is the nature of the divine rule for which John the Baptist gave his life?

The persistence of the crowds is another cause for concern. Jesus needs some time alone without the distractions of the crowd to think through these questions about God's rule. So he takes a boat across the Sea of Galilee to a "lonely place." But the crowd sees him leave and anticipates his intentions. They scramble by land over the north shore of the sea, and when Jesus does land, they are already there. Apparently they picked up numbers as they raced to meet Jesus. Matthew says they "came after him in crowds by land from the towns." So when Jesus steps off the boat, he finds that his plan has been thwarted, that he will not get the solitude he had hoped for.

II

At this point Matthew makes a telling comment that is our first clue why this story was so widely circulated among first-century Christians. When you or I have our plans thwarted, we usually respond with anger, frustration, and resignation. But Matthew says that when Jesus saw the crowd, "his heart went out to them, and he cured those who were sick." "His heart went out to them"—not anger, not frustration, not resignation, but compassion. The crowd is thoughtless and heedless of the consequences of their impetuous action (as the rest of the story shows). They don't ask themselves why Jesus was trying to get away, and they don't ask how they will take care of their own physical needs in this lonely place. All they know is that they've got a good thing in this Jesus, and they don't want to let him slip through their fingers. Jesus responds with patient compassion. He temporarily gives up his own desires and needs in order to minister to the desires and needs of these thoughtless people. What an attractive, winsome person this Jesus is.

The crowd is a large one—five thousand men, "to say nothing of the women and children," Matthew tells us at the end of this story. Among them are many who are sick, who come to Jesus with their need, and Jesus heals them. All of this takes time. Evening comes on. No one has had anything to eat. The disciples become concerned and advise Jesus to dismiss the crowd so that they can go into the nearby villages to buy food. This suggestion sounds reasonable. But when we consider that the crowd is large and the villages are small (it is, remember, a lonely place), we see that the disciples' suggestion is not such a good one after all. It could produce chaos, and people could get hurt in the scramble for food. So Jesus says there is no need to send them away. Instead, he instructs the disciples to "give them something to eat yourselves." They must be perplexed at this command. Does Jesus think they anticipated this problem and made provision to feed such a crowd? Is Jesus telling them to share whatever food they may have brought with them? In either case, it's a silly thing for Jesus to say, and their response indicates how woefully inadequate Jesus' solution to this problem is. "All we have here, " they say, "is five loaves and two fishes." (These loaves are not our loaves. They are flat, round pieces, more like a hard pancake than a loaf of Wonder Bread.) "All we have are these meager provisions, so we can't possibly do what you want," the disciples are saying.

"Give them to me," Jesus says. He takes the loaves and fish, blesses them, breaks the cakes of bread into bits, distributes the pieces to his disciples, and they in turn distribute the bread to the crowd. Matthew doesn't say so, but we can assume that Jesus distributes the fish in the same way. Matthew does say that "everyone ate to their hearts' content." In fact, there is so much food that the disciples gather "twelve great baskets" full of leftovers. It is now almost dark. Jesus sends the disciples away to the boat and dismisses the crowd. Having been fed, they can now make the journey back to the towns and villages from which they came. At last Jesus has the solitude he had been seeking. He goes further up the hillside to pray alone, and night falls. The crowds are on their way home, Jesus having ministered to all their needs. The disciples are in a boat on the Sea of Galilee. Jesus is alone on the hillside praying.

III

That is Matthew's version. Mark's is essentially the same, except that he contributes many details that make the story all the richer in its implications. One difference between Matthew and Mark is the reason for Jesus' withdrawal to the lonely place. In Mark, the disciples have just returned from their first "evangelistic crusade," which Jesus had commissioned at the beginning of chapter 6. Mark interrupts this narrative with the story of John the Baptist's murder, then returns to it when the disciples rejoin Jesus and report on their mission, which was very successful. They had driven "out many devils, and many sick people they anointed with oil and cured" (Mark 6:13). Jesus listens to their reports, then says, "Come with me, by yourselves, to some lonely place where you can rest quietly." In Mark, Jesus' motivation is to give the disciples some quiet time to reflect on the nature of their discipleship. In Matthew it is danger that calls for such reflection, but in Mark it is success.

As in Matthew, the plan to get some privacy fails: ". . . many saw them leave and recognized them, and came round by land, hurrying from all the towns toward the place, and arrived there first." Luke identifies the place as being near a town called Bethsaida on the northeast shore of the Sea of Galilee. Jesus had been preaching and teaching and working miracles in the vicinity of Capernaum on the northwest shore, so this boat trip cuts across the northern edge of the sea. The boat may have always been in sight of the shore, and that may explain how the crowd knew where it would land. Whatever the explanation, in Mark as in Matthew, Jesus steps out of the boat to find a large, expectant crowd; and as in Matthew, Jesus' heart goes out to them. But Mark gives a reason for Jesus' compassion—"they were like sheep without a shepherd, and he had much to teach them." This crowd is undisciplined and very much in need of what Jesus can give them.

The day wears on as Jesus teaches the undisciplined crowd the things they need to know. The disciples become concerned because it is getting late, and this is a lonely place. They come up to Jesus with a reasonable request: "Send the people off to the farms and villages round about to buy themselves something to eat." As in Matthew, Mark reports that Jesus responds with the command for the disciples to provide food. And as in Matthew, the disciples remonstrate. But Mark elaborates on their objections: "Are we to go spend two hundred denarii on food for these people?" they say. This is a rhetorical question. They don't have two hundred denarii, which represents an enormous sum to the disciples. One denarius equals about twenty cents and represents approximately one day's pay for a common laborer. Not even two hundred days' income would be sufficient to feed this crowd. Mark gives us this figure in order to heighten the incredulity of the disciples and the greatness of the miracle.

IV

The citation of the monetary figure also demonstrates something else—namely, that the disciples still don't understand who Jesus is and what he can do. When Jesus commands them to provide food, their solution is to see if they can raise enough money to go to the grocery store. Remember that in Mark's account the disciples have just returned from their first mission in which they performed many wonderful acts. Jesus is serious when he tells his disciples that they can provide food for so many people. They have been healing people and casting out demons. Why should they not be able to meet this need as well?

Whatever Jesus' intention, the disciples show no confidence in being able to do what Jesus requests, so Jesus asks them to do something that is within their natural abilities—take an inventory of what food is available. They report back that there are five loaves and two fish. (John's Gospel tells us that the food came from a young boy present in the crowd, not from the disciples' resources.) Then Jesus commands them to do something else within their capabilities—organize the crowd in one hundred rows of fifty each on the green grass. Now this unruly mob is ordered and disciplined. Jesus takes this little amount of food, looks up to heaven, blesses it, breaks the bread and distributes it to the disciples, who pass it on to the people. All these people become linked together in the distribution. Jesus gives the bread to the disciples, the disciples give it to the persons on the ends of the rows, and the persons on the end pass it down the rows. They repeat the process with the fish. Each time a disciple returns to Jesus, having distributed these elements, he finds even more to give to those who have not yet been served.

These simple elements—five loaves and two fish, a common laborer's food for one day, which is capable of feeding one or possibly two people—become multiplied over and over again until all have eaten "to their hearts' content." This meal of simple, common food satisfies everyone. There is, in fact, food left over—twelve baskets full of broken bread and fish, one basket for each of the disciples.

All four Gospels mention the twelve baskets of leftovers, and it should be clear that all four intend to convey something more than just a literal truth in mentioning this detail. A basket for each disciple. Why, then, were there twelve disciples? The first Christians saw themselves as the new Israel, the successors to the old Israel. The disciples represent this new people of God, this new Israel; and the number twelve is one way this reality is conveyed. The people in the crowd, by accepting this gift of food, become, at least for the moment, members of this new community. The twelve baskets symbolize this reality. (John's Gospel casts a different, darker light on the whole miracle. It reports that the crowd tried to seize Jesus to make him king, but that Jesus anticipated the crowd's reaction and escaped to the hills.)

In this new Israel there will be enough for everyone. The Synoptic writers have an Old Testament story in mind as a reference for this miracle. It is the story of Elisha's miraculous provision of food in a time of famine (2 Kings 4:42-44). Elisha and the sons of the prophets are living together trying to make do, when an unnamed man comes to them with a virtual treasure of food—twenty barley loaves and some fresh grain. The problem is that there are over one hundred men to be fed. Elisha says to his servant, "Give to the men that they may eat." (Jesus' command to the disciples is virtually in the same words.) Elisha's servant objects. In effect, he is saying, "How am I to do that?" "Are you crazy? People are starving these days, and just to put this food down in front of a large, hungry group who can't all have some of it is to invite big trouble." But Elisha insists because "thus says the LORD, 'They shall eat and have some left.' " And Elisha was right.

Jesus has less to work with and far, far more to feed. So clearly one greater than Elisha is here.

V

Who is Jesus, then, this one greater than Elisha? There is a Jewish tradition that when the Messiah comes, he will inaugurate the messianic age with a banquet for all of his people, for Israel. This banquet will be a celebration in which all who participate will be satisfied. Matthew, Mark, and Luke present the feeding of the five thousand as this messianic feast and Jesus, therefore, as the Messiah. Or, if this is not the feast itself, then this incident is an anticipation of the feast that will come when the messianic age finally arrives in all its fullness. In either case, the Gospels present Jesus as the Messiah, as the one who fulfills all the hopes and longings of Judaism. (John's Gospel, characteristically, gives this incident a different twist. He says it occurred about the time of the Passover, implying that Jesus is the Passover lamb, slain for the salvation of Israel.)

But if this is the messianic banquet of Judaism, it is also something else, something specifically Christian. Bread and fish often appear in early Christian frescoes as symbols of the Eucharist, the symbolic and sacramental meal all Christians share in commemorating the life, death, and resurrection of Jesus. John's Gospel uses bread as a symbol for Christ (who is the "bread of life"). And one of the Greek words for fish, *ichthus*, became an acronym for Christ (each of its letters standing for one word in the formula "Jesus Christ, Son of God, Savior"). This banquet of common people on common food is a foretaste of the Eucharist, the "good gift" all Christians share with one another each time they partake of the Lord's Supper. Christ offers this food in the same way he offers his life. The bread and fish Jesus gives the five thousand sustains them on their journey home, and without this food some of these who are "like sheep without a shepherd" might be lost. The bread and wine of the Christian Eucharist sustains Christians in their journeys through the world. And without this spiritual nourishment, we would be lost. Physical and spiritual nourishment are here, and not just nourishment but extravagance—there is more than enough food here to satisfy body and soul. Jesus Christ, Son of God, Savior is the Eucharist, God's good gift to us, which nourishes and sustains us spiritually.

We are like that crowd that chased Jesus around the north

shore of the Sea of Galilee. We are undisciplined. We are hungry for something and think that Jesus can supply it. But as John's account shows, we probably don't understand who Jesus is, and we probably misunderstand what he will do for us. We want him to be a wonder worker who will solve all our problems for us. He wants to be a nourisher who gives us the strength and discipline to solve our own problems. We come to him confused, unsure, selfish, short-sighted, thoughtless—caught up in our own concerns, some important but most petty and trivial. He takes us as we are and patiently and compassionately begins turning our small potatoes into a wonderful feast. The real miracle of the feeding of the five thousand is the spiritual transformation of the crowd from the self-seeking, leaderless mob with no concern except for itself and with a clamoring desire not to let this Jesus get away (he's too good to be true) into disciples (at least for the moment). Jesus is too good to let go of, but not in the sense the crowd thinks. Jesus gives the crowd something it hadn't bargained for, but something far better than it had bargained for. Jesus gives the crowd nourishment that will sustain them even when he is not physically present. And that is why Jesus can dismiss them, why they go back to their towns and villages willingly, no longer clamoring to keep Jesus in sight lest he get away. He *is* still with them, though he is no longer with them.

Every time Christians worship, especially when we gather around the Lord's table in the memorial he established, we experience the miracle of the feeding of the five thousand. Jesus nourishes us with his presence, then dismisses us back to our "towns and villages" to be his disciples. In the act of worship, Jesus becomes present even though he is absent. It is no wonder, then, that the four evangelists told and retold this story.

The Syrophoenician "Dog"

Matthew 15:21-28

I

There are a few stories about Jesus in the Gospels that shock and puzzle us. They present Jesus in uncharacteristic ways. In these stories he says and does things that just don't sound or look like what we've come to expect. The cursing of the fig tree during Jesus' last week is one of these stories. And the exorcism of the Syrophoenician woman's daughter in Matthew 15 is another. This particular miracle shocks us because Jesus seems so harsh, insensitive, even cruel to this woman in need. His treatment of her seems so out of character. First, he ignores her; then he says his healing powers are for Jews only (since she's a Gentile—a Syrophoenician according to Mark, a Canaanite according to Matthew—she need not apply for assistance); then he calls her a "dog." All of this is very troubling. Why would Jesus, usually so compassionate and alert to others' feelings, treat her this way? This story seems to have implications for the question of racial prejudice and ethnic stereotypes. The only problem is that Jesus is the one apparently guilty of the racial slur!

As always, the first step in understanding such a narrative is to see it in context. Jesus has just engaged the Pharisees in a controversy concerning the Jewish laws of defilement. The Pharisees and lawyers have criticized Jesus for not making his disciples wash their hands before eating. This criticism angers Jesus, and he lashes out at his critics for putting the law above human need. The religion of the Pharisees is a "lip-service" religion, Jesus says, quoting the prophet Isaiah. Instead of understanding what God intends, the Pharisees have put their own erroneous interpretation on the law. And their error is not primarily an intellec-

137

tual one. It is, rather, a moral one because it makes them overlook human need. This criticism leveled at Jesus and his disciples is such a petty matter. If the Pharisees really think that this sort of thing is what matters most, then they have missed the point of their faith.

So if religion is not a matter of external obedience to a set of rules and regulations, what is it? "Listen to me and understand this," Jesus says, "we are not defiled by what goes into our mouths, but by what comes out of them" (Matthew 15:10-11). Religion has to do with what you are within, in your innermost reality, what you are in secret, as Jesus says in another place. Religion has to do with the intangible realities of who we are—our attitudes, intentions, purposes, motives, desires—as much as it has to do with external behavior. Our external behavior is an indicator of our inner spiritual reality. So, for the Pharisees to jump on Jesus for not requiring his disciples to wash their hands as a religious act prescribed by the law and for them to pass over the good things Jesus is doing indicate they are in serious spiritual trouble.

II

What Jesus teaches about the importance of the spirit in religion has radical implications for the Jews. If observance of the law in its external details doesn't really count, if it is what comes from within that really matters, then couldn't anyone with the proper spirit, the proper inner being and attitudes, come to God? And if the answer is yes, then what need is there of the law? And if the law is not really necessary, then what need is there of Pharisees to set an example and lawyers to interpret cases? And (perhaps even worse) if the law is not really necessary because the inner spirit is what really counts, then couldn't even Gentiles come directly to God without having to conform to the law's strictures? Jesus is playing with fire here. This teaching threatens to strike a spark in the tinder of Jewish/Gentile relations and start a conflagration that will consume all that Jews hold dear.

This is why the disciples come to Jesus in private and say, "Do you know that the Pharisees have taken great offense at what you have been saying?" (Matthew 15:12). Jesus' anger at the Pharisees has not abated, so his response is full spleen. "Any plant that is not of my Father's planting will be rooted up. Leave them alone; they are blind guides, and if one blind man guides another, they will both fall into a ditch" (Matthew 15:13-14). The Pharisees' religion is not anything God planted and cultivated, Jesus says. Their religious instruction and counsel are about as reliable as the guidance of one blind person for another.

Given Jesus' testy mood, Peter might have done better to keep quiet. Peter has many endearing qualities, but sensitivity and quickness of wit are not two of them. "Explain this parable," Peter says. "We don't understand what it means." What a blockhead Peter is! If we had been there, we would have understood what Jesus was saying, wouldn't we? (In fairness to Peter, he is asking this question on behalf of all the disciples, none of whom seem to have gotten the point.) "Are you still as dull as the rest?" Jesus responds. In effect, he says, "Are you no better than the Pharisees who have missed the point? Whatever we take into our bodies cannot defile us or harm us spiritually. But what comes out of our mouths—that is, our words and deeds—show what we really are inside because they come from the heart. The evil deeds that we do proceed from our inner spiritual reality. And that reality is what can defile us."

This whole controversy must have been very discouraging to Jesus. Neither the Pharisees nor the disciples seem to understand. The Pharisees should understand because they are the experts in the law. But their very expertise seems to be the thing that blinds them. And one would think by now that the disciples would have begun to understand something of what Jesus was about. Instead, all they see is that Jesus has offended the Pharisees. It's as if the disciples think that Jesus doesn't know he's offended them and, now that he does know, he will stop.

III

In this angry and discouraged state of mind, Jesus decides to "withdraw"—to leave Jewish territory altogether, to get away from the likelihood of confrontation with the Pharisees. He therefore leads the disciples into the region of Tyre and Sidon. I think we must visualize the following scene: Jesus out ahead of the disciples, determinedly heading up the road into pagan territory, the disciples lagging behind, not exactly sure why they are following such a strange and bewildering leader. After they enter this pagan land, a subtle drama plays itself out which will reinforce the point Jesus has tried to make about the importance of the spirit. And this drama will also, incidentally, restore him to a better humor.

This drama begins when a Canaanite woman comes "crying out" after Jesus and the disciples. The *out* may refer to the *crying*, or it may refer to the *coming*, or it may refer to both verbs. The woman is crying out as she comes out. In other words, this woman's house is beside the road down which Jesus is traveling; when Jesus passes by, she comes out of her house and cries out after him. We don't know how she knew about Jesus. All we know is that she needs help and believes he is the one who can help her. "Have pity on me, Son of David," she cries. "My daughter is tormented by a devil." And here Jesus makes the first of his puzzling responses. He ignores her. "But he said not a word in reply," Matthew says. He continues right down the road. But the woman isn't to be put off by this snub. She follows after Jesus, yelling out her need.

Well, this is an extremely embarrassing situation for the disciples. Miss Manners would not approve. Here they are in a pagan land with a strange pagan woman following them, yelling at them. Jesus doesn't even seem to notice. Finally the disciples become so embarrassed that they catch up to Jesus and beg him to do something. "Send her away; see how she comes shouting after us," they say in their embarrassed desperation. At this point I think Jesus stops, turns, and confronts the disciples. Then he makes the second of his puzzling responses. "I was sent to the lost sheep of the house of Israel, and to them alone," he says. The literal meaning of these words is this: "My mission is to Israel, and to Israel alone. My teaching and my powers of healing are for Jews only, not for people like this pagan woman." Is this literal meaning Jesus' intended meaning?

Perhaps, but there are some indications that Jesus is speaking ironically. For one thing, these words address the disciples, not the woman. She has been following behind them and catches up only after Jesus has spoken these words. So if Jesus is addressing the disciples, what is he saying to them? Their embarrassed request, remember, was to "send her away." In other words, the disciples simply assume that Jesus won't want to have anything to do with this woman because she is both a foreigner and a woman. The disciples are guilty of both racial and sexual discrimination. They would never come right out and say that they don't want to have anything to do with her because she's non-Jewish and a woman. So Jesus simply says out loud what the disciples are thinking but are too polite to voice. Jesus is not really concerned with the woman at this point. Rather, it's his disciples who concern him, because their attitude toward the woman indicates they don't really understand how she should be treated. So Jesus says aloud what the disciples are thinking silently in order to confront them with their prejudices.

IV

This confrontation between Jesus and the disciples allows the woman to catch up with them, fall at Jesus' feet, and repeat her request. "Help me, sir," she says. She is probably out of breath because of her strenuous pursuit, so she cannot relate the whole story. All she can do is make the simplest, most heart-rending plea for help. "Help me, sir." I think Jesus has known all along what he is going to do. He will grant her request. No one who has come to Jesus in need and in faith has ever been turned away. So why, then, does Jesus do the third puzzling thing in this story—apparently put the woman down by calling her a "dog"? He says, "It is not right to take the children's bread and throw it to the dogs." Literally this means: "I am meant for Israel, not Gentiles; and so compared to the Jews, you are little better than a dog." I suspect the disciples wince when Jesus says this. One doesn't say things like that in public, even if one thinks them. But that is the point. If one really thinks that, shouldn't one be willing to say so publicly? If the disciples are embarrassed to say out loud what they are thinking, then maybe there's something wrong with their thinking. Once again, Jesus says out loud what the disciples silently think in order to confront them with their prejudices.

The woman's response is masterful. She will not be put off by this apparent racial slur. Why does she persist in the face of this apparent put-down? Perhaps she is so distraught by her daughter's condition that she doesn't notice or doesn't care. Perhaps her shamelessness so far emboldens her, so that Jesus' shamelessness in slurring her simply doesn't matter. Perhaps her desperation is such that Jesus is her last hope, so she has to persist in spite of this inauspicious response. Perhaps, since she shows herself to be a woman of quick wit and sure intelligence, she senses that Jesus is not really speaking to her but rather to the disciples and that he is trying to teach them something. Whatever the reason, she comes out with an inspired rejoinder: "True, sir, and yet the dogs eat the scraps that fall from their masters' table." She is saying, "Maybe I'm just a 'dog' in comparison with the Jews, yet even our pets get some consideration. We don't begrudge them the scraps that fall to the floor. I'm not asking for the whole loaf of bread, only for a scrap."

And now, I think, for the first time, Jesus directly addresses the woman instead of his disciples. And now, for the first time, his words are in character; they sound like what we have come to expect from him: "Woman, what faith you have! Be it as you wish!" (And at that moment, Matthew says, this woman's daughter was restored to health.) Jesus is full of admiration for this woman. She has understood something that neither the Pharisees nor his own disciples have understood. It is faith that counts. It is that inner sense that God is willing to grant our deepest desires if only they are legitimate and if only we persist in believing in God against all obstacles. Here again, as with the Roman centurion, we have a foreigner and a member of a despised class (a woman) who understands what is really important, while the disciples fail to see.

V

And now we should recall the context of this story—the controversy over what makes us clean or unclean, over what enables us to come into God's presence and what excludes us from God's presence. Jesus had said that external things, such as washing your hands, can't possibly keep you out of God's presence. But internal things, such as your attitudes, purposes, and intentions, can exclude you. These are inside of you and come out of you in what you say and do. And if they are unclean, they will surely cut you off from God.

The disciples' inner reality is fear, embarrassment, and prejudice. These spiritual qualities defile them, make them unclean, and keep them away from God and out of the kingdom. It is of little consequence whether or not they wash their hands before eating because at the rate they are going, they are not going to make it into the kingdom. Here these disciples have been with Jesus constantly these past months, and they still don't see. But this woman— a perfect stranger, who never ever set eyes on Jesus until this moment, much less ever listened to his teaching—this woman has the kind of faith that gets her heart's desire. This woman has the kind of inner reality that makes possible communion with God. It doesn't matter that she's pagan and that she's a woman. All that matters is her faith. What comes out of her doesn't defile but rather purifies. Her faith makes her clean. She demonstrates what really counts. She will be in the kingdom and have her heart's deepest desires filled.

It appeared that no one had understood what Jesus was getting at. And that angered and discouraged him. But then, unexpectedly, from the most unlikely of persons, someone demonstrates exactly what Jesus had been trying to teach. So Jesus commends the Syrophoenician woman with words of high praise. He restores her daughter to health. But *she* restores his good humor and confidence. The Syrophoenician woman proves that we do make a difference, for good or for ill, to God.

Falling Walls, Scoliosis, and a Lesson in Gratitude

Luke 13:1-17

I

Many of Jesus' healing miracles have to do with phenomena we encounter today but call by names different from those used in the Bible. Matthew says the two Gadarene wild men were demon-possessed; we say they were criminally insane. The Syrophoenician woman's daughter was "tormented by a devil"; we say the process of her socialization was not going well. The miracle in Luke 13:1-17 concerns a woman who was bent double, "quite unable to stand up straight." She was "possessed by a spirit that had crippled her for eighteen years," Luke says; we say she was suffering from scoliosis or curvature of the spine. Perhaps our medical and sociological jargon is more accurate than the biblical terminology of evil spirits. The reality of these afflictions, however, is the same quite apart from the terms we use.

People in the ancient world also had an insight we are just recovering today—namely, that there is a connection between physical health and spiritual states. Luke says it was a spirit that crippled this woman. He doesn't say it was the spirit of the woman herself that caused the crippling. Perhaps it was a negative spirit from her parents. Or perhaps she had had a brutish husband who abused her in various ways. We don't know the etiology of her disease. All we know is that a spiritual malady was one of its primary sources.

Luke's comment that a spirit was the source of her problems connects this healing with the immediately preceding teaching

144

of Jesus. Some otherwise unidentified people told Jesus about an incident that presumably had only recently occurred. Pilate, the Roman procurator of Judea, had mixed the blood of some Galileans with their (the Galileans') sacrifices. It is difficult to know exactly what happened, though it clearly was horrific. Apparently some pilgrims from Galilee had offered sacrifices in the Jerusalem temple, and in so doing they had somehow run afoul of the Roman authorities, who slaughtered them on the spot.

Whatever the incident was, Jesus takes the story to imply that these Galileans must have been guilty of some terrible sin, so that their terrible fate was a just punishment. Jesus counters this implication with his own story of eighteen people who were killed when the tower of Siloam fell on them. "Do you imagine," Jesus asks, "they were more guilty than all the other people living in Jerusalem?" Do you think, in other words, that these people were greater sinners than the rest of Jerusalem so that they, and only they, deserved such a fate? "No," Jesus says, "I tell you they were not; but unless you repent, you will all of you come to the same end." We're all equally guilty or equally innocent. These awful incidents could happen to any of us.

II

Jesus, of course, doesn't literally mean that government authorities will slaughter us at worship or a wall will fall on us and crush us to death if we don't repent. What he means is that without repentance we will suffer a terrible fate (which these physical calamities merely symbolize). This is why Luke places the parable of the fig tree immediately after the debate about these incidents and immediately before the healing of the woman with scoliosis. This parable illustrates the nature of the danger we all face if we fail to repent. The true danger to our well-being is spiritual, not physical.

Here's the parable.

A man had a fig tree in a vineyard which his gardener had tended and cultivated for three years. Yet there were no figs, so the owner told the gardener to cut the tree down and plant something that would produce fruit. But the gardener pleaded for the tree to be given one more chance. Then, if another year of cultivation didn't bring results, he would cut the tree down.

This is a parable of judgment. And the judgment on the fig tree has to do with its failure to perform its function—namely, produce figs. This tree has had enough time and nurture to begin producing fruit. It is failing to fulfill this purpose, so it might as well be dead. Of course, it's possible that this tree fulfills other worthwhile purposes. Perhaps it gives shade to the vineyard workers when they take a break. Perhaps it is pleasing to behold and the mere sight of the tree refreshes both workers and passersby. These considerations, however, are secondary to the main one—that the tree was planted to produce figs, and that it is failing. The judgment to cut the tree down rests on this fact.

Jesus is saying that we are like the fig tree. If we don't fulfill our main purpose in being, then we might as well be dead. And if we go long enough without producing fruit, we will eventually shrivel up inside and die spiritually. The awful fate of being slaughtered in the very act of worship or being crushed by a falling wall is symbolic of this spiritual death. In order to avoid such a fate, we must fulfill our essential purpose in being. And doing that rests on our first repenting. If we repent, then we will begin producing fruit, that is, fulfilling our reason for being. If we don't repent, though, we will eventually die, no matter how useful we may be in other ways. In the same way that the tree may have been good for other purposes than the main one, we may be good for purposes that miss the main point. And these other purposes are not sufficient to keep us from perishing. (Jesus is also warning us that we are in serious spiritual danger if we think that physical death is the worst thing that can happen to us. These stories of death are terrible, but it's far worse to live a long life and miss life's point. We don't tolerate unproductiveness in our agriculture. Why should God tolerate that in us?)

III

If missing the point of life can produce such dire consequences, what then is the point of life? Jesus' parable, with its frightening implications, moves this debate about whether or not suffering and death are judgments on sin from the academic and intellectual level to the existential. If something worse than physical death can happen to me because I miss the point of life, then how can I begin to understand life's purpose and begin to live it out? Jesus' teaching has raised this disturbing question, and it is at this point that Luke inserts the story of the woman with scoliosis. Apparently Luke sees this miracle as an answer to the question about the purpose of existence and the nature of the fruit we are to bear.

The first thing to say about this woman is that she cannot fulfill her human purpose in any real sense because of her deforming illness. Whatever the purpose of life is, this woman does not exemplify it. That is, if we were to ask, "Where can we find a good example of what human beings were created for?" we would not point to this woman. She lives a marginal life in every sense. Think, for example,what her physical life must be like. She is physically deformed and probably in constant pain, or at least in constant discomfort. Her physical state limits her ability to make a living. It denies her meaningful work. But even if she has some skill—she's an expert seamstress, say—who will buy her work? Her deformity, remember, is attributed to a spirit; and after the healing, Jesus himself says she was "Satan's prisoner." Most people consider her a sinner, a person being punished for sin; and it's probably better not to have business dealings with such a person. Or social relations, either. Perhaps charity is required toward her, but it would be unthinkable to befriend her or invite her into one's home. Even her spiritual life is deformed. Though allowed into the synagogue, she is only allowed on the fringe (as we shall see).

This woman's physical deformity deforms every other important aspect of her existence—her work, her relations with others, and her spiritual life. If this skewed character of her existence vividly illustrates what life is not supposed to be, then it also illustrates what life is supposed to be. God created us to be physically healthy and whole, to have relationships of mutual care, concern, trust, and support, and to be rightly related to God.

When Jesus sees this woman in the synagogue one sabbath, he calls her up to him. It is important to catch the implication of Jesus' calling this woman to him. Jesus is teaching in the synagogue, which means he is the center of attention. The woman, in contrast, is at the fringe of the congregation; that's why Jesus has to call her to him. She is allowed into the synagogue, but only at the back, on the fringe. Like the hemorrhaging woman, this woman is marginalized. Her place in the synagogue illustrates her standing in society. Jesus calls her from the fringe to the center, and then he does two things: he speaks and he acts. "You are rid of your trouble," he says. Then, he lays his hands on her (perhaps on her curved, bent-double back), and immediately the woman stands up straight, cured of her illness.

IV

This woman had been suffering, but now the cause of her suffering is gone. In some ways she is like the Galileans and Jerusalemites who suffered (though, of course, her suffering had not yet killed her). Now, she has been delivered. And now we recall Jesus' warning that a terrible fate awaits us if we don't repent. Has this woman repented? Is something worse than her physical deformity about to befall her? What does repentance have to do with this woman and her condition (both her illness and her cure)?

We normally think that repentance has to do with sin after the fact. I sin. I repent. You sin. You repent. This story suggests, however, that repentance may have more to do with basic attitudes than with acts of contrition. That is, this story suggests that true repentance may be an attitude of mind that constantly discerns and resists temptation, even before we yield and even if we don't yield. This woman has been delivered from one danger, but now she faces a greater and more subtle danger. Has she been saved from physical perishing only to perish spiritually? Think for a moment how this woman might have reacted to the miracle that cured her.

Bitterness: Look at all those wasted years. Eighteen years I was afflicted! Look at all the things I've missed; my life has been ruined. Why did this happen to me at all? Why couldn't I have been cured sooner?

Self-centeredness: Look at all the joys and pleasures I've been denied. I'm not going to lose any more time. I'm going to start right now to make up for lost time. I'm going to start right now to experience all the things I've missed!

Melancholy/Apathy: Well, yes, I'm fine for now, for the time being. But I really can't count on such things lasting. I was ill once, and I'll probably get sick again. There's no point in feeling happy about this (I'm glad, of course) because I know it won't last.

Instead of these reactions, Luke tells us she "began to praise God." She is thankful for her deliverance and does not dwell on those lost years or get totally absorbed in herself or become depressed by the possibility of future suffering. She is grateful for what had happened to her, and she recognizes the source of her healing. She praises God. She avoids (at least for the moment) the spiritual perishing that threatens us all. She is in no danger (as is the fig tree of the parable) of being rooted out and destroyed. She has the attitude of repentance because in the moment of her healing she has successfully resisted these temptations. She will not suffer the fate Jesus warned about as a possibility for us all if we don't repent.

V

There's another character in this story who doesn't come off too well—the president of the synagogue, who becomes indignant at this healing. His objection is not that the woman was healed, but that Jesus healed her on the sabbath in violation of Jewish law. His point is that there are other times when Jesus could have performed this act. This was not an emergency, and Jesus could have waited. We ought not to assume that this man was not glad the woman was healed. Rather, his anger comes from the fact that Jesus could have waited one more day without violating the law.

Jesus counters by arguing that the law allows work that is necessary on the sabbath. He draws an analogy. On the sabbath everybody unties dumb animals from the manger so they may be watered. Why should not this woman be freed from her constraints on the sabbath as well? The analogy is not a perfect one because the animals are presumably in good health, and their health might be impaired if they were forced to go one day a week without water. The woman, in contrast, has been in ill health for some time, so it is unlikely that one more day of suffering would be all that detrimental to her. If Jesus claims to be a spiritual teacher and leader, how can he set aside one of the fundamental requirements of the law?

It's a good question. Whenever anyone claims spiritual insight, yet acts outside the established norms, we need to be careful. We need to weigh their claims to spiritual truth on an exacting scale. The synagogue president is right to point out that this act violates the sabbath law. His error, however, is in the conclusion he draws from this fact—that the woman's healing should have been delayed. The proper conclusion is this: There's something wrong with our understanding of the sabbath if it forbids us to alleviate suffering.

Jesus, on another occasion, established the proper principle with regard to religious rules and regulations when he said, "The sabbath was made for humans, not humans for the sabbath." In other words, human need takes precedence over religious law. The law about keeping sabbath holy is a very good one. But it's not good if we misunderstand it so that we become insensitive to human need. If we put regulations before compassion, we are in grave spiritual danger. The president of the synagogue is precisely in such danger because he has his priorities mixed up. Instead of rejoicing in the woman's restoration to full health (with all the implications it has for her relations with others and God), he attacks Jesus. He says, "You shouldn't have done this no matter how good and compassionate and kind it was, because the law says no work on the sabbath."

And at this point we need to remember the debate about the Galileans and the Jerusalemites and the parable of the fig tree. People who suffer (like this woman) are not necessarily sinners, and sinners (like this synagogue president) don't necessarily suffer. Indeed, sufferers may have more spiritual insight than respected members of the community (who may in fact be sinful). All of us—sufferers and sinners alike—need to repent or something worse than physical suffering may befall us. We may become subject to spiritual insensitiveness. And if we do, we will begin to perish spiritually because we have missed the most important thing.

The woman who was bent double has the attitude of repentance, which enables her to avoid succumbing to the temptations her healing raises. She responds with gratitude and thankfulness, not bitterness, self-centeredness, or melancholy. The ruler of the synagogue, in contrast, does not have the attitude of repentance. He responds to her healing with indignation. He has, in this most crucial encounter, missed the point.

Blind Bartimaeus

Mark 10:32-52

I

The four Gospels record the miracles of Jesus primarily to teach something about Jesus and our relationship to him. The miracle stories, in other words, are theological in nature rather than historical or biographical. They proclaim that Jesus is the Messiah, and they illustrate the nature of what believing in him involves. This last miracle we will consider is no exception. The healing of blind Bartimaeus is a parable of discipleship, which Mark indicates by the way he opens and closes this narrative. His opening words are: "They were on the road, going up to Jerusalem, Jesus leading the way; and the disciples were filled with awe, while those who followed behind were afraid" (Mark 10:32). His closing words are: "And at once he [Bartimaeus] recovered his sight and followed him on the road" (Mark 10:52).

The disciples and the rest of the crowd are following Jesus on the road to Jerusalem. But it is an uneasy kind of following. The disciples are in "awe," and the crowd is "afraid." Why is Jesus so set on going to Jerusalem? Why does Jesus forge ahead in such an intense and determined manner, so that everyone else has trouble keeping up with him? The scene Mark sketches with these brief opening words is one we've all played out. Someone we know and care about seems tense and preoccupied, and we don't quite know how to approach him or her. Do we try to say something? Do we just act normally, as though nothing is wrong? Do we fall into silence and let our friend or loved one broach the subject?

The disciples opt for this third choice, and Jesus doesn't disappoint them. In every miracle story we've considered so far,

Jesus has shown his awareness of and sensitivity to what those around him are thinking and feeling. His manner has disturbed the disciples, so he draws them aside to tell them why he is so intense and preoccupied. They are on the way to Jerusalem, he says, and Jerusalem represents his final appeal to the Jewish people. Jesus knows this appeal will fail. He will be rejected, and he knows what that rejection will mean. The highest authorities will condemn him to death, then turn him over to the hated Romans, who will mock, spit on, flog, and kill him. Death at the hands of the Romans means death by crucifixion. And all of the disciples have witnessed enough crucifixions to understand why Jesus is preoccupied.

But, Jesus says, three days after this awful death, the Son of Man will rise again. The end of this story is resurrection, not death.

II

The disciples must have heard the part about resurrection but not the part about mocking, flogging, and death. They illustrate the great capacity of the human mind to block out unpleasant information and let only what is pleasing through. Immediately after Jesus spoke these somber and prophetic words, James and John, two of his closest disciples, take him aside to make a request in private. When this resurrection occurs, they say, and you have come in all your glory, we want to sit on your right hand and your left. The image James and John use is that of a king, seated on his throne, with his closest advisers and next in authority on either side, ready to decide the affairs of state. We want you to declare, they are saying, that we are the next in authority to you in this kingdom you are about to inaugurate.

Given the gravity of what this journey to Jerusalem represents and the almost total failure of comprehension this request demonstrates, Jesus responds in a remarkably gentle way. Perhaps he has come to realize that the disciples (even his closest ones) will never fully understand him until after Jerusalem and the Passion. He says, "You do not understand what you are asking." And then it occurs to Jesus to find out just how far their understanding does go. So he asks, "Can you drink the cup I drink, or be baptized with the baptism I am baptized with?" "Drinking the cup" was a popular expression for enduring some kind of trouble or unpleasantness. And "baptism" in this context means being immersed or overwhelmed by waves of misfortune—as in being crucified. James and John respond, "We can"—fateful and perhaps fatal words because Jesus says, "So be it. You will drink my cup and suffer my baptism."

When Jesus said this, I think James and John may have brightened up. They had approached Jesus with some trepidation—what if he refuses? But his assertion that they will share his suffering must mean that he is granting their wish. Whatever unpleasantness this "cup" and "baptism" represent, it will be nothing but a necessary and relatively insignificant prelude to their accession to power. However, if they are elated, their good feeling doesn't last long because Jesus then goes on to say something else. "I can't promise you the exalted seats of authority you request," he says, "because they are not mine to give. Someone else will make that decision." James and John must have been flabbergasted by this turn of events. What kind of kingdom is this that the king can't even pick his own advisers? Worse, they have committed themselves to some unspecified unpleasantness, yet have failed to get what they want. And on top of that, the other ten disciples get wind of their request and get mad at them. Their anger at James and John is self-righteous indignation mixed with self-recrimination. I have no doubt that every one of them was saying to himself, "How could they have done that! The very idea! How could I have let them beat me to the punch that way!" I have no doubt that all of the disciples dreamed of being second in command to Jesus, just like James and John.

Once again Jesus calls his disciples aside and patiently tries to teach them exactly what their discipleship means. "You know that in the world the recognized rulers lord it over their subjects," Jesus says, "and their great men make them feel the weight of authority." What a nice image he uses—"the weight of authority." We talk about people "throwing their weight around" and mean the same thing. All of the disciples had this unholy desire to throw their weight around in Jesus' kingdom. But this is not the way it is supposed to be in this kingdom, where the king doesn't even choose his own advisers. Instead, Jesus says that "among you, whoever wants to be great must be your servant, and whoever wants to be first must be the willing slave of all." Then he says, "Look at my own example. The Son of Man did not come to be served but to serve, and to give up his life as a ransom for many."

III

As Jesus approaches the end of his journey to Jerusalem, he is confronted by a blind man, the beggar Bartimaeus, son of Timaeus. Bartimaeus lives in Jericho, a city a few miles northeast of Jerusalem. Jewish pilgrims from Galilee to Jerusalem usually crossed over the Jordan River in Galilee to its eastern bank, traveled down the east side of the river until opposite Jericho, then crossed the river again and passed through Jericho. The reason for this roundabout route—instead of going directly south from Galilee to Jerusalem—was to avoid passing through Samaria, whose inhabitants the Jews despised. Jesus follows this route with the crowd of Passover pilgrims. And now, having passed through Jericho and having begun the last leg of his last journey, Jesus encounters Bartimaeus, a blind man.

Bartimaeus is beside the Jerusalem road, crying out for alms. He is a professional beggar, and this Passover time is his Christmas season. He knows that a crowd of religious people on pilgrimage is a good crowd for a beggar to work. As a professional, he is undoubtedly good at reading crowds, so it is not surprising that he picks up on the specific interest of this particular pack of pilgrims—namely, that one among them, a certain Jesus of Nazareth, may be the Messiah. Bartimaeus must have heard this kind of talk before in Passover crowds. I'm sure he is skeptical, that he knows messiahs are a dime a dozen. But it doesn't really matter to him whether or not this Jesus is the Messiah. All that matters at first is that the crowd believes it. Bartimaeus knows that if he can get the blessing of this Jesus, his take for the day may be very good indeed.

So he cries out, "Son of David, Jesus, have pity on me!" At first the crowd is annoyed and tries to silence him, but their opposition only spurs the beggar on. He calls out all the louder, "Son of David, have pity on me!" Jesus stops—yet another journey interrupted by a cry for help. "Call him," Jesus says. He will see what this blind beggar wants. When the crowd sees that Jesus is willing to deal with Bartimaeus, it starts singing a different tune. "Take heart, he is calling you," someone says. Perhaps everyone senses that something dramatic is about to happen. Perhaps at this moment the thought first runs through Bartimaeus's mind that there may be something to the crowd's enthusiasm for Jesus. Perhaps he thinks, *What if this Jesus is the Messiah? What if this time there's really something to it?*

We don't know what went through Bartimaeus's mind, but we do know what he did. When he hears that Jesus of Nazareth, putative Messiah, is calling him, he throws off his cloak, springs up, and comes to Jesus. William James once wrote something to the effect that we don't run away because we're afraid, but that we're afraid because we run away. I don't think Bartimaeus springs up because he believes. It may well be the case that he comes to believe because he sprang up. Whatever state of belief or disbelief he may be in psychologically, his behavior betrays belief. First, he throws off his cloak. The cloak is the outer garment, a long single piece of cloth covering most of the body. To throw it off is to disencumber oneself, to strip for action, to get rid of that which might impede one. So, disencumbered he springs up—that is, he doesn't merely get up, he jumps up, he scrambles to his feet. There's an expectancy and eagerness in his action, and also probably no little fear. He may be wondering just exactly what he's let himself in for by calling attention to himself. But whatever it is, he's willing to risk it. He gropes his way through the crowd, which makes way for him, and finally stands face-to-face with Jesus.

IV

If Bartimaeus is doing a daring thing by coming to Jesus, Jesus is doing a daring thing in asking him to come. The crowd will expect something spectacular now. Other messiahs have dropped a few coins in the tin cup and blessed the beggar. But for Jesus to ask Bartimaeus to stand before him is to ask for trouble. What if Bartimaeus asks for something more than alms? Asks for something Jesus can't give? This large crowd, so enthusiastic for Jesus now, will disappear like the morning mist if Jesus can't deliver.

Jesus compounds this audacity with another. He asks the beggar, "What do you want me to do for you?" Surely it would be much safer to use the occasion for a short homily on the patient enduring of suffering or perhaps a diatribe against the inadequate social services provided by the Romans (who allow poor, blind beggars to roam the streets of Judea's cities). Instead,

Jesus practically invites some impossible request by asking what Bartimaeus wants of him. The most natural thing to expect a blind man to ask for when face-to-face with the Messiah would be his sight. Jesus, however, doesn't assume he knows what Bartimaeus wants, and his question demonstrates his deep understanding of the human heart. He knows that if you've lived with a disability for awhile, you may have developed ways of coping with life that will be hard to change. It might be scarier and more difficult to have your sight back than to continue in your blindness. So he asks, simply and directly, "What do you want me to do for you?"

How swiftly this narrative moves! How quickly an encounter with Jesus can alter the terms of our existence! What does Bartimaeus want from Jesus? What do any of us want from Jesus? At the beginning Bartimaeus is nothing but a beggar working a crowd, wanting and expecting nothing more than alms. He's like everyone else beginning a new work day. Another day, another dollar. But then he senses a promising angle; and when he starts to play that angle, the whole thing gets out of hand and mushrooms into a field of possibilities he never dreamed of. Now he must make a decision. There's no time for calm, rational consideration of the alternatives. What *does* he want? And is the one confronting him with this question able to grant whatever it is he wants?

Perhaps Bartimaeus did not know himself until he opened his mouth, what would come out. Perhaps Bartimaeus has the strange experience of hearing himself talk, as if it were someone else saying it. He says, "Master, I want my sight back." It's such an audacious, incredible thing to ask for that perhaps he can't believe his ears as he hears the words. But as soon as the words are out of his mouth, he knows they're the right ones. What he wants above all else is to see again. And something else happens in that moment when he begins speaking. The way he addresses Jesus changes. At first he used a formal messianic designation, "Son of David." His use of this term did not necessarily mean he believed Jesus is the Messiah. He could, after all, have been playing to the crowd. But standing face-to-face with Jesus, confronted with the possibility that this one might be the Messiah and also with the question of what he really wants, Bartimaeus says, "Master." He may not have meant to say "Master." But once he says it, it's too late; it's already out. And—if not before he said it—after he said it, it becomes the truth.

V

However unpremeditated and unintended and impulsive this commitment may be, it is enough for Jesus. "Go, your faith has cured you," Jesus says. And with these words Bartimaeus recovers his sight. Jesus makes no demands on the beggar. He simply says "go"—go back to the life you were living before you became blind. Go on your way; you're free to choose now how to live. I've restored you and released you. It's your life once more. And with that free choice to do whatever he pleases, what does Bartimaeus choose? He chooses to follow Jesus on the road that leads to Jerusalem.

This journey to Jerusalem, where Jesus will confront the "recognized rulers of the world" and be put to death by them, began with a mysterious event we call the Transfiguration. Jesus had taken Peter, James, and John with him to the top of a high mountain. There Moses and Elijah appeared with Jesus, and Jesus' cloak began to shine with a dazzling whiteness which "no bleacher on earth could equal." (Matthew compares this brilliance to the brightness of the sun.) The brightness was so great that the three disciples had to be protected from going blind by a cloud that cast a shadow over them all. This visual spectacle was accompanied by a voice out of the cloud that said, "This is my Son, my Beloved; listen to him" (Mark 9:2-8).

Surely with manifestations like these, the disciples must see and understand who Jesus is. And they do have flashes of insight when (almost by accident, it seems) they understand something of the truth about Jesus. But these moments of insight are all too rare. All too often the disciples hear but don't hear, see but don't see. Beginning with the Transfiguration, the Gospels subtly play with the theme of blindness versus sight. Jesus' controversies with the Pharisees represent one kind of blindness—the blindness of obstinacy, the refusal to see the light. The disciples' persistent failure to understand Jesus is another type of blindness—the blindness, perhaps, of being too close to the light. Either too much darkness or too much light can make us blind.

Perhaps the people in these miracle stories who have encountered Jesus are at the best advantage to see who he really is and respond in faith. Their deep need for help, at times bordering on desperation, enables them to see through the niceties and obligations of the Pharisees' traditions. And, since most of these encounters are first encounters with Jesus, they can perhaps see Jesus in a fresh way the disciples can't. Bartimaeus is the blind man who can "see." The disciples are the sighted ones who are "blind." Bartimaeus sees Jesus as one who can make him well. The disciples see Jesus as one who can make them powerful.

Above all, Bartimaeus sees Jesus as one who can save him. That is why, when he is free to choose what to do with his life, he chooses to follow Jesus into Jerusalem. Here, the contrasts stop, because the disciples, for all their blindness, have made the same choice. Once in the midst of a terrifying storm on the Sea of Galilee, they cried out, "Save us, Lord!" And Jesus saved them. And that was enough. No subsequent failures to see entirely put out the light this experience cast on Jesus and on them.

There is no problem or risk or danger Jesus has faced so far that he has been unable to master. Wild storms at sea, the even wilder storms within the human heart, and death itself (the strongest, most terrifying enemy of all) have yielded to his peremptory presence. The leper, the Roman centurion, Peter's mother-in-law, the Gadarene demoniacs, the woman with the hemorrhage, Jairus, the leaderless crowd of five thousand, the woman of Syrophoenicia, the woman with scoliosis, and now blind Bartimaeus—all encountered Jesus in their need, and Jesus helped them. He more than helped them, he saved them. And so they all in their own ways followed Jesus, even to Jerusalem.

We too encounter Jesus in our need and in our hope. And Jesus says to us, as he said to all these others, "What do you want me to do for you?" If we ask for it, he will give us our sight back, perhaps not in an instant, as with Bartimaeus, but gradually, as with the disciples we follow Jesus to our own Jerusalems.

DATE DUE

AP 23 '98			
DE 10 '99			

DEMCO 38-297